BESIDE THE SHADBLOW TREE

Beside the Shadblow Tree

A Memoir of James Laughlin

HAYDEN CARRUTH

COPPER CANYON PRESS

Printed in the United States of America.

Grateful acknowledgment is made to Galen Garwood
for the use of his artwork on the cover of this book.

The publication of this book was supported by grants
from the Lannan Foundation, the National Endow-
ment for the Arts, and the Washington State Arts Com-
mission. Additional support was received from Elliott
Bay Book Company, Cynthia Hartwig, and the many
members who joined the Friends of Copper Canyon
Press campaign. Copper Canyon Press is in residence
with Centrum at Fort Worden State Park.

LIBRARY OF CONGRESS
CATALOGING-IN-PUBLICATION DATA
Carruth, Hayden, 1921–
Beside the shablow tree: a memoir of James Laughlin
/ by Hayden Carruth.

p. cm.

ISBN 1-55659-099-7 (alk. paper)
1. Laughlin, James, 1914–1997   2. Literature publishing
– United States – History – 20th century.
3. Publishers and publishing – United States –
Biography.   4. Carruth, Hayden, 1921– – Friends
and associates. 5. Poets, American – 20th century –
Biography.   I. Title.
PS3523.A8245 Z63 1999
881'.54 — dc21   99-6160
CIP

9 8 7 6 5 4 3 2
FIRST PRINTING

COPPER CANYON PRESS
Post Office Box 271
Port Townsend, Washington 98368
www.ccpress.org

CONTENTS

BESIDE THE SHADBLOW TREE

FOREWORD
BY SAM HAMILL

It is impossible to imagine what twentieth-century American literature might look like without the luminous presence of James Laughlin (1914–1997). As founder and publisher of New Directions, he was responsible for a list that began with the high moderns, Ezra Pound and William Carlos Williams and H.D., and included literally hundreds of this century's greatest writers from across the world. In his eulogy printed in *The Nation* (December 15, 1997), Eliot Weinberger wrote, "Laughlin was more than the greatest American publisher of the twentieth century: His press *was* the twentieth century."

Laughlin founded New Directions while still a student at Harvard. He had been to Italy to visit Ezra Pound and attended what he and Pound dubbed "the Ezuversity." Looking over Laughlin's youthful poems, Pound suggested that young James could contribute more to literature by using his wealth – Laughlin's family were Pittsburgh steel barons – to publish literature than by taking himself too seriously as a poet. The consequences of his decision shaped this century's literature while Laughlin himself became a unique and remarkable poet and memoirist.

For most of his life, Laughlin didn't publish his own poetry except for a few tiny pamphlets and books privately printed in limited editions and mostly given to literary friends. He told me in a letter, "Pound always claimed, and told me as his publisher, that what mattered to him was being read by the 'seven right people.'" But in the last two decades of his life, as though finally convinced by the likes of Hayden Carruth and many other trusted poets, Laughlin released a veritable deluge of poetry including *The Bird of Endless Time, The Owl of Minerva, The*

Secret Room, The Collected Poems, a *Selected Poems,* and several others. His memoir of Pound, *Pound as Wuz,* is a minor classic. His published letters to and from Ezra Pound, William Carlos Williams, Kenneth Rexroth, Henry Miller, and Thomas Merton provide a portrait of Laughlin as editor, publisher, friend, and patron of several of this century's giants. His generosity was renowned.

He could also be cold, aloof, irascible, self-serving, self-mocking, humble, and utterly charming. He warned me during the early years of Copper Canyon Press that being an editor-publisher isn't easy or often rewarding – everyone second-guesses your decisions, he said, and everyone, both those one publishes and those one doesn't, complains. Carruth verifies Laughlin's observation, "I also discovered in the files [of New Directions] what vile egomaniacs some writers can be, people who heaped contumely on Jas's head and on anyone else's head on the staff of New Directions... and in spite of these vitriolic attacks on him his efforts never wavered." He was sometimes elegantly simple and often frustratingly complicated. But his integrity was beyond question.

Carruth, in his brilliant introduction to Laughlin's *The Collected Poems,* quotes from a letter from the poet: "What my poems are about is the juxtaposition of contemporary life with ancient cultures." The same may be said of Laughlin's life. Schooled in the classics at Choate and Harvard, he became the most Latin of all our poets. Even while publishing the avant-garde, his patronage of literary arts was modeled on classical patronage: *noblesse oblige.* His dalliances with young women he referred to as his *apsaras,* "divine nymphs" in Hindu mythology, were embarrassingly legendary.

If James Laughlin was a model of a the cosmopolitan literatus, his old friend and colleague and sometime editor, Hayden Carruth, is an inexact opposite – poor, reclusive, struggling with severe chronic depression. Despite profound differences in their personal lives, poetry specifically and literature in general provided grounds for an intimate friendship spanning more than fifty years.

Hayden Carruth's *Beside the Shadblow Tree* is not meant to be a definitive statement on James Laughlin. It will require volumes to gain the broad portrait required of such a man. It is a recording of the meditation of one great old poet upon the death of another, one with whose life his own intertwined in various ways for half a century. The author did not research names and dates and places. Late in his meditation he writes, "Should I go back to the beginning and rewrite this memoir to make it more accurate? That is what Jas would have suggested. He was a stickler not only for accuracy but for tidiness. But this is my work, not his. I could and did mimic his style in language, though not in other things, when I needed to, but my own poetry and prose were always naturally different from his, to say the least. This is a matter of esthetic, not moral, judgment. To my mind the value of the kind of writing I'm doing here, if it has any, is in its spontaneity, its closeness to the actual mental flow, which is a virtue that Jas did not appraise highly. I will leave this thing the way it is."

Carruth can be every bit as self-deprecating and as obstinate as Laughlin. At one point, following his hospitalization in a mental ward, he calls himself "a man completely defeated by the world – who was nevertheless venturing into the world again." His courageous venturing has rewarded us with a huge body of celebrated poetry and prose. In a footnote he writes, "If I were a historian rather than a sedentary old man brooding on his past, I could go to the records." To which I would counter that it is precisely because it *is* Carruth's utterly candid meditation, his memoir of James Laughlin and himself, that this book is so moving. Historians will order the facts.

BESIDE THE SHADBLOW TREE

In 1951, or thereabouts,[1] I moved from Chicago to New York and went to work for an outfit named Intercultural Publications, Inc. We called it simply Intercultural. It was a small corporation, chartered in the state of New York as a not-for-profit, part of the huge effort after World War II to restore a style of harmony and goodwill to international life – a sort of literary and artistic Marshall Plan – and it was funded by a sizable grant from the Ford Foundation, which had its headquarters in Manhattan. The person who hired me, the person who had been responsible for launching Intercultural and securing the subsidy, was James Laughlin, whom I called Jas.

At that time office space was hard to find in the big city. Intercultural was lodged unconventionally in a suite on the second or third floor of the Hotel Pierre on Fifth Avenue, overlooking the park, kitty-corner from The Plaza, both of which I could see from my office windows. A strange place. Often the lobby would be crowded with guys in big hats who spoke with a drawl and whom we called the oil millionaires. Maybe they were, maybe they weren't, but there's no doubt that men of that type favored the Pierre in those days, and we at Intercultural felt a little uncomfortable in their midst. But we fared well anyway. My office was a good-sized room with three windows overlooking the avenue, a couch, a private bathroom, a big desk, an Oriental carpet, chairs, etc. Next to it was an even larger central room which accommodated three women, Hannah Kaufman, who was my secretary, Mary Coxe, who was a general assistant, and another who spoke with an English accent and was secretary to

1. I'm writing this entirely from memory. No research. Conditions are not the best.

Jas, and whose name escapes me.[2] Then beyond the central room was Jas's office, similar to mine except that his windows looked out on 59th Street. In the back was a kitchen, a storage room, and I don't remember what else. It was a snug enough office. And when I wanted to spend the night there I simply called the maid and asked her to make up my couch for sleeping. I kept a razor and toothbrush in the bathroom.

Intercultural was in the business of promoting international cultural exchange. We were the first, for instance, to bring Ravi Shankar to the United States, also the Balinese dancers. We sent exhibitions of American painting, including people like Ben Shahn, Jackson Pollock, and Rockwell Kent – I worked to put them together with the help of a wealthy woman who lived on upper Park and had at least a million dollars' worth of paintings on her walls, though again I forget her name[3] – to Europe, Africa, and South America. But our biggest and most demanding project was the publication of a quarterly magazine called *Perspectives USA*. Each issue was edited by a different distinguished American writer or critic, and although some original material was included, most of the contents were reprinted from American literary magazines and quarterly reviews. *Perspectives* was well, not to say lavishly, produced, with original artwork for the covers and plenty of full-color reproductions inside. Once chosen, the contents of each issue were translated into French, German, and Italian by teams of translators in

2. Please do not think that because my memory is failing in old age I have, or had, any less regard for those whose names have deserted me than for those whose names haven't. I remember the Englishwoman well; she was a strong and likable presence in the office. If this were a scholarly dissertation rather than an informal memoir, i.e., if I were a historian rather than a sedentary old man brooding on his past, I could go to the records and find her name easily.

3. I think it was Peggy Guggenheim.

Europe, and four editions – English as well as the others – were produced over there and distributed around the world. For purposes of copyright a small edition was also produced in this country, but no attempt was made to distribute it. The idea was to make American art, writing, and criticism as widely available as possible, and at the same time to help serious American periodical publishers by paying good fees for permission to reprint materials from their pages. The translators were mostly poets and fiction writers who needed a little help too. Everyone benefited, or at least that was the aim.

This was an extraordinarily ambitious undertaking. Jas hired me to be "co-ordinator," and that was my official title. I spent by far the larger part of my time and energy on *Perspectives*, though I attended to other projects as well. It was a daunting job. I dealt with widely scattered editors, writers, artists, and translators, and with printers and binders in England, The Netherlands, Germany, and Italy. I set up – at this point I've no idea how – a network for international distribution. But the problems were often far beyond my range of competence. What do you do, for instance, when half a carload of finished magazines disappears in transit from Madras to Calcutta, or when a hundred copies are impounded by customs in Australia or Argentina? I had no experience in such matters, nor did more than a few other people at that time. I sat in my office in the Pierre and thumbed the yellow pages constantly for experts who could help me. Fortunately money was not one of my problems. I had nothing to do with the budget. As far as I in my humble station could tell, the source of funding was unfathomable.

Jas took care of all that. He was on close terms, apparently, with Bob Hutchins, Ping Ferry, and others who had been associated with the Center for the Study of Democratic Institutions

9

in Santa Barbara and were now consultants at the big Foundation, guiding its policies in the sectors of artistic and intellectual affairs.

Jas was tall. I don't remember how tall, but I'd guess now he was 6′4″ or 6′5″, and like many tall people, especially then – i.e., before basketball became popular – he stooped a little when he was standing. When he walked he went slowly with a modified shuffle. He had injured his back rather seriously in a skiing accident in New Hampshire when he was young, which may have accounted for the stoop, though I'm inclined to think he would have stooped anyway; it went with his temperament. He deprecated his tallness, and complained because he couldn't walk through a normal doorway or sit in a normal car. In the office he was a quiet presence, yet always noticeable if only because he smoked cigars. The aroma lingered in the rooms and halls, and the women said they liked it. He preferred a Cuban cigar, double claro with a candela wrapper, such as could be obtained easily in those days before the embargo, good cigars that I generally couldn't afford; but from time to time he would give me one. And to tell the truth, when I was working late I sometimes stole a cigar from the box on his desk, though I was primarily a cigarette smoker. When he spoke his voice was quiet, a mid-baritone with no discernible regional accent. His speech was the standard American speech of the midwest, which certainly includes Pittsburgh, his native city. I remember several occasions when he was speaking French with someone from France and he wanted me to take notes about some arrangement or other he was making: I couldn't catch some of what the Frenchman was saying, but I could understand Jas easily, because he spoke French with a decided American, almost a schoolboy's, accent – fluently but flatly and with full articulation. Later on, when I read his poems written in French, which he called his "Frenchies," I came to appreciate how he had turned his

Americanized French into a special and very expressive poetic language by combining it with elegance of sentiment in the great erotic tradition.

But during that time in the early fifties, Jas was often not in the office. This was the period of his most intense interest in Asian life and culture; he made extended trips to India, Ceylon, Burma, and Thailand, and at New Directions he published a good many books about Asian civilization, such as a translation of Henri Michaux's *A Barbarian in Asia* and that book about Burma by the Englishman Collis, a program which culminated, perhaps, in Tom Merton's *Asian Journal,* edited by Jas after Tom's death. Jas traveled everywhere and brought home huge collections of Asian artifacts – paintings and small bronzes, some of which were on display in his office, but other things too. He brought me a silk tie once from Rangoon, which he called a Thai tie.

Jas traveled with a portable Dictaphone. He used it on airplanes, in hotel rooms, wherever he was, and sent back great numbers of Dictaphone reels to be typed up in our office by the Englishwoman, chiefly memos to me. Instructions and notes, suggested solutions to problems, messages to pass on to editors and writers, but also often observations of local people and landscapes or anything else that caught his eye. For years Jas relied almost exclusively on the Dictaphone for conducting his correspondence, and like others who have done the same he fell into the error of volubility. His letters and memos were too wordy. When you occasionally received a letter written in his own hand or on his little portable Royal typewriter, you saw at once how much more succinct his real literary style could be. And when I saw how much time the Englishwoman was putting into these memos, I told her to quit typing the Dictaphone reels, and instead to let me listen to them on her machine while I took notes. It saved a lot of work.

When Jas was in New York during this period he lived in a small apartment somewhere in the midtown area – East 50th Street or somewhere like that. Not long after I moved from Chicago he had a party for me there to introduce me to friends and others who might be useful. But I was so nervous that I drank too many martinis and became drunk, no doubt disgracing myself and Jas too. Yet he never complained about it. I never saw him drink too much himself, though he liked a good wine and favored cognac with his after-dinner cigar, but he had a great tolerance for others who drank too much – or took too much dope – especially if they were poets.

My first duty at Intercultural, the first morning I reported to work, was to accompany Jas to the French consulate on Fifth Avenue where he was awarded the *Légion d'honneur* for his work in publishing French literature in America. The ceremony was held in a library, a small but elegant room with many bookshelves along the walls. I think Bob MacGregor from New Directions and I were the only American observers, joined by a small gathering of French dignitaries. We were each given a glass of champagne. The consul made a speech and proposed a toast, to which Jas responded in his somewhat stilted French, and we all raised our glasses. Bob, however, was on the wagon; he merely wet his lips and set his glass on the edge of a bookshelf, whereas I swallowed my wine in two gulps and looked around for more. There wasn't any. So I took Bob's glass and finished it off.

Jas said nothing to me about the honor he had been paid by the French government. In his remarks during the ceremony he was altogether self-effacing. That was the beginning of my understanding of Jas (to the extent I ever understood him at all): in spite of everything he had done, the many famous people he had known, all his hard work and success, he was pathologically – and I mean this literally – shy. Many aspects of his life and sensibility can be explained, if too easily, by his constant embarrassment and his attempts to disguise it.

My own pathology was a lifelong neurotic anxiety, about which I've written quite enough elsewhere. It determined everything in me. It made me, not similar to Jas, since I lacked his force entirely, but sympathetic to him, and it was particularly evident at that time. I was feeling awful. I was in therapy with a pleasant but restrained Austrian woman who had known Jung, which meant that although Intercultural paid me more than my employer in Chicago had, I still was relatively poor. Psychotherapy is the privilege of the leisure class, as we know. It is also the ball and chain of the toiling proletariat. Nor, for that matter, did the Austrian lady help me much. I used alcohol to make life possible, to give me the strength I needed for my new role in the sophisticated world of New York, and like all alcoholics I believed this was veritably the only way. It was. I drank a martini every morning for breakfast and carried a bottle of gin in my briefcase. The folly of this is apparent to anyone, of course. Yet to this day I know for a fact that I could not have done what I did without the booze.

Even with the booze I couldn't do it for long. I worked for about a year or a little longer at the Intercultural office, at which point I could do it no more. Jas was sympathetic (though he never expressed any reaction to my illness, for or against it). He kept me on the payroll and assigned me tasks I could perform at home, writing essays and reviews, editing manuscripts, doing ad copy and blurbage, and this continued for perhaps half or three-quarters of a year. During that time I wrote an extended essay about Ezra Pound, using some of Jas's memories, and it was published in *Perspectives* and republished in a number of European countries, Poland, Czechoslovakia, etc., in translation.

It was an instructive rather than analytical essay, but many writers, including Pound himself, thought it was pretty fair literary criticism. A modest success. And then the inevitable final crisis arrived, which precipitated me into the loony bin. My connection with Intercultural was ended.

◇◇◇

After dinner at Meadow House.[4] One of Ann's dinners: soup to nuts with candlelight and finger bowls, a little bell to summon the maid with. Jas is standing behind Ann's chair with a new cigar in his hands. As he picks off the little shreds of tobacco to open the end of the cigar he throws them into Ann's hair. At first she doesn't know what is happening, but then she does. "James, how could you?" she says in a loud voice. She jumps up and runs out of the room.

◇◇◇

Why did Jas hire me to come from Chicago and join him at Intercultural in New York when so many other qualified people were already on the scene? I never knew. I was too shy to ask, and I guess Jas in his different way was too shy to say. But this was the psychological context in which our relationship evolved for many, many years to come.

At that time he scarcely knew me. We had met in 1948 or 1949 during the hullabaloo over the awarding of the Bollingen Prize to Ezra Pound for his *Pisan Cantos*. At first it seemed as if the imbroglio would pass away without any big consequences, but then when Norman Cousins and the *Saturday Review* chipped in, and hired Robert Hillyer to write his series of attacks on

4. The Laughlin residence in Norfolk, Connecticut.

14

Pound, the Bollingen Committee, and the modernist movement in poetry generally, bringing in the HUAC[5] and other redneck elements on their side, it became serious. I was editor of *Poetry*, the monthly magazine in Chicago that had been established in 1912 by Harriet Monroe to publish and promote new poetry in America. I felt that *Poetry* was the logical agency to undertake a counterattack against Cousins and Hillyer. I went to New York and conferred with various members of the Bollingen Committee – Louise Bogan, Allen Tate, Léonie Adams, and others – and at the same time I called up Laughlin, who was Pound's publisher, and suggested that we might join forces. We met in a dark basement restaurant somewhere in the Village near the New Directions office, which at that time was on 6th Avenue. As I descended into the restaurant I saw a tall dim figure rising, almost unwinding, at one of the tables. I knew it must be Laughlin. He came forward and introduced himself and took me back to his table, where he introduced his friend, Gertrude Huston.[6] We had dinner. The talk was lively, lubricated with martinis and wine, punctuated with laughter. I wish I could reproduce it, but I can't. We talked about what might be done to muster support for Pound and the Committee,[7] and at one point I remember Jas saying, "We must get Tom to help us"

5. The House Un-American Activities Committee, chaired at that time, I believe, by Representative Cox.

6. Gertrude was an artist who at that time worked as designer and production manager for New Directions. Many years later she became the third Mrs. Laughlin.

7. The Committee consisted of the fellows in poetry at the Library of Congress, though this may not have been their official designation. They comprised about a dozen. All of them voted for Pound's book to receive the prize except dramatist Paul Green and Karl Shapiro, who said he couldn't vote for a poet who was an acknowledged anti-Semite. In the end the Committee was disbanded and the Bollingen Prize was withdrawn by its sponsor, the Mellon Foundation, from the auspices of the federal government and given instead to Yale University.

– meaning, of course, T.S. Eliot in London – whereupon he went off to find a phone and send a cable. (Naturally Eliot responded with a statement in support of Pound, but in the end we didn't use it.) I don't remember how our dinner concluded or even where I was staying at the time. What I do remember is that we were incensed with Hillyer's ignorant and malicious attack on Pound and Eliot, New Directions and *Poetry*, and we were enthusiastic about making a substantial rebuttal. But a few days later we decided that neither New Directions, as Pound's publisher, nor T.S. Eliot, as the focus of Hillyer's libel, should participate in the rebuttal, since to do so would create an appearance of self-interest. The rebuttal was left to *Poetry*, i.e., to me, and a while later I published a pamphlet called *The Case Against the "Saturday Review of Literature,"* which contained essays and statements by a good number of prominent American poets and which attained a substantial circulation.

Between that dinner in the basement restaurant and my arrival in New York several years later I did not see Laughlin. Whatever communication we had was by letter and phone. In 1949 or 1950 I left the editorship of *Poetry* and became an associate editor at the University of Chicago Press. A year or two after that I became sick of Chicago and wanted to leave; I was not a native Chicagoan, since I came from the east, and I was going through the breakup of my marriage – it was a difficult, depressing time. Perhaps I let my feelings be known to Laughlin somehow, I don't remember. But at some point I received his offer of a job at Intercultural, probably in a letter (because neither he nor I cared much for the phone), and I accepted it eagerly.

We hadn't seen each other for quite a while. We had no working relationship. I was too tied up and otherwise distracted to write much at that time, only an occasional book review for *The Nation* or a little poem for one of the quarterlies. We had no personal relationship either, as far as I can recall. We must have kept in touch a little, but we had no regular correspondence. All Laughlin knew about me was that I had some knowledge of publishing, some facility for editing. But so did many other young people of that time, including writers whom he knew well and whose books he had published at New Directions. Nevertheless, he offered me the job. I didn't know why then, and I don't know now. Nothing beyond the merest practical details of work was ever discussed between us. And as awkward as it may seem, for fifty years our friendship was conducted in precisely this tacit, impersonal manner.

◇◇◇

One time at Intercultural we were discussing literary critics who might be of use to us, probably as editors of individual issues of *Perspectives*. I suggested Van Wyck Brooks. "That old whore!" Jas said immediately. I knew enough not to press the matter, and partly I agreed with him. Then another time, ten years later in Norfolk, we were wondering which literary elder might be suitable for... I don't remember what we had in mind, probably an editorial job of some kind, or perhaps only an endorsement. Jas suggested Van Wyck Brooks as blithely as if he were suggesting his own uncle.

The editorial mind is nothing if not flexible. The good editorial mind, that is.

◇◇◇

In 1953 when I entered Bloomingdale, the hatch in White Plains where I remained for nearly a year and a half, my connection with Intercultural was over, although the program there continued for a number of years and was expanded to include special sections in *The Atlantic Monthly* devoted to different foreign contemporary cultures and literatures. I don't remember who was hired to take my place or when the program was suspended and Intercultural was put to rest.[8] I lost touch with everyone there except Jas. Occasionally a little piece of Intercultural business would still crop up, as when I received a note from Paul Goodman saying he found it peculiar that none of his poems had appeared in *Perspectives* – Paul being ever a diligent self-promoter. I wrote back on a Bloomingdale letterhead: "Paul, there are a lot of peculiar things in this world." Certainly my own predicament was peculiar, locked up behind bars among loonies of every status and condition. I felt as alien as a frog on an iceberg – yet I knew I was where I had to be. Jas kept in touch. Never obtrusively; he did not visit or send long letters of sententious advice, as others did. But from time to time I'd receive a little note of encouragement, or a box of fine cigars would arrive at the hospital from Dunhill's or Sherman's in the city. Usually his letters would contain requests for help of some kind, editorial advice or jacket copy for a particular book New Directions was publishing, and this was his way: he never expressed concern for another directly – or if he did it was merely pro forma – but always indirectly and usually in terms of some objectifiable need of his own. I learned in time that this was the characteristic mode of all his hundreds of benefactions. When he paid Kenneth Rexroth's rent or bailed Gregory Corso out of the pokey, he did it impersonally, through some third person or some established agency. He didn't want to talk about it, or even to acknowledge what he had done.

8. On paper it may still exist.

My sojourn at Bloomingdale, including the electroshock, the hydrotherapy, and all the rest, did me no good whatever, and later I was told that my emotional problems were unamenable to treatment in a hospital and that I should never have been a patient in the first place. Thanks a lot, I said. I left the place toward the end of 1955 and went to live at my parents' house in Pleasantville, New York. I lived there in total seclusion for about five years. I had agoraphobia, claustrophobia, acrophobia, and every other phobia known to man, concatenated in a generalized fear of reality in all its social and metaphysical aspects. To the extent that I could, I supported myself by doing freelance editorial work, depending for assignments on former colleagues and relatives in the business, especially my brother Gorton, who worked for McGraw-Hill, and Paul Corbett at Harcourt, Brace and Fred Wieck at the University of Michigan Press. I don't remember all I did: reading and copyediting manuscripts, ghostwriting, producing catalog copy and flap copy for new books, etc. At one point I was even typing book manuscripts at ten cents a page for a vanity publisher in New York. Once you were in the network, the loop, such jobs came without much effort on your part, if you were willing to work cheap – as I was. I did jobs for New Directions during this time, but I don't recall what they were. Other jobs that came to me may have also originated with Jas, such as the translations from French that Elisabeth Borgese of the *Encyclopaedia Britannica* commissioned at that time; I never knew for sure, but I suspected it. I kept more or less busy, and I earned enough to give my parents something for my keep. It was a dismal time for me, of course, and a complicated time, but this is not the place for a detailed discussion of it.

I was helped immensely by a wonderful psychiatrist from White Plains, Peter Laderman, who was not attached to the hospital, though he was recommended to me by one of the interns there, and who was willing to come to see me at my home once a week.

Toward the end of the five years I began to circulate in the world again, at least a little. I could go riding in a car, for instance, if anyone would take me. I could walk in the high-school playground behind my parents' house, though I still couldn't walk on the street in front of it – too many houses, too many windows staring at me. After quite a while of this, I summoned enough courage to take the driver's test and have my license renewed, one of the most momentous things I've ever done, and eventually I bought a car, a thirdhand MGA. It was a blessing. I had many hairy moments in that car, many panics, but at least I was mobile, especially at night. I could and did drive all over the countryside in the darkness, though I never got out of my little car and never put the top down. Eventually I even drove to Peter Laderman's office in White Plains; I parked the car, I walked to his building, I rode the cramped elevator to his floor, I sat in his waiting room with other patients – no one will ever know what this cost me, though Peter has a better idea than anyone else.

Then Jas wrote to me and asked if I'd be willing to go up to his place in Norfolk and straighten out his collection of little magazines. He would pay me something for the work and put me up. This was out of the blue, very surprising, and I said yes.[9]

I drove to Norfolk, I found Meadow House (which is on Mountain Road near the edge of town), and Jas greeted me. So did his wife Ann; they had married a year or two after I got out of the hospital, I think. Ann was tall, a little taller than I, which befitted the wife of James Laughlin, a somewhat austere-looking woman with red hair and an angular face, but very pleasant,

9. As nearly as I can recall this was in the winter or early spring of 1960.

very eager to welcome me and make me comfortable. I was put into the guest room, which had its own bath – and strange window shades that you pulled from the bottom of the window toward the top. I'd never seen anything like them before. In fact I'd never seen a house quite like Meadow House either. It wasn't a mansion, it wasn't opulent or overbearing, but it was large – about fifteen rooms, I think – and it was, to say the least, very comfortable. The living room, which looked out over a gently declining meadow with a clump of white birches in the center and a flock of sheep scattered over the turf, was also large, probably thirty feet long and twenty feet wide, with a big fireplace in which a fire was burning, many bookshelves crowded with Latin and Greek texts, an original seascape by Marin on the wall and a Magritte on the opposite wall, a huge philodendron (which was called Elihu Root), a couple of sofas, an assortment of chairs and tables, lamps, etc. It was – and is – a pleasant, well-lighted, well-used room, so liked by Jas that he made it his office while he was at home and had a desk in one corner next to a big window overlooking the meadow with a television set not far away, on which he could watch the Pittsburgh Pirates while he worked on his stamp collection or dictated letters.

Jas took me up to the attic and showed me the magazines, hundreds of them, including many famous magazines from the old days: *The Little Review, transition, Vortex,* etc., shelved in long rows against the unfinished attic walls but obviously not in good order. Jas wanted me to straighten them out and make a catalog, preparatory to donating them to a university library, probably Harvard or Yale. Then the next day Ann and Jas left for New York where they had an apartment in the Village on Bank Street, and I was left alone in the big house.

Alone except for Wonza. She was the cook. She not only fed me, she served me, as I sat by myself at the big table in the dining room. This was for me the strangest aspect of life at Meadow

House. I'd never before had anything to do with a servant. The word itself was repugnant, and the whole idea embarrassed me. Yet at the same time I was anxious and ignorant, and didn't know what to do, so I sat at the table and said nothing while Wonza, in her dark dress and white apron, ministered to me. It took me a couple of days to venture into the kitchen and speak to her. Wonza was an African-American woman, as we say nowadays, who had come originally from Florida and had served on the staff at Aunt Leila's mansion before transferring to Meadow House. She was a strong woman, a little portly though not much, with a lined face and graying hair. She knew I felt awkward and self-conscious, and she spoke casually to me and tried to put me at ease. She succeeded, at least to some extent, and in the course of time Wonza and I became very good friends.

◇◇◇

Even though I never met her and know little about her, Aunt Leila was a distinct presence in Norfolk, as she still is. In hundreds of ways her importance to Jas is manifested all the time. First, the geography. She lived on an estate called Robin Hill which she and her husband had established in Norfolk long before I met Jas. The estate consisted of perhaps 1,000 acres of woodland on the north side of Canaan Mountain, centered around a mansion on a knoll beside Mountain Road. The house was huge; I don't know how big it is, but I've been in most of it and I'd guess at least fifteen rooms, probably more. Aunt Leila and her husband built it, or had it built, in 1929 in the mode of Edwardian splendor, with dark woodwork predominating indoors, many small recessed windows that admit a modicum of daylight, gold-plated fixtures in the bathrooms, plenty of dark-looking plush furniture. Outside was a beautiful garden on all sides of the mansion, with terraces, flower beds, hedges, stone walks, Renaissance Italian statuary and pottery, and an abundance of flowers at all times during the growing season, beginning with a massed display of azaleas and rhododendron and laurel in the spring. Mountain Road is a small country road leading from Norfolk to the top of Canaan Mountain, which is the highest elevation in that region but not much of a mountain by other standards. At the top is a lake which serves as a reservoir for the village. The road is paved from Norfolk to as far as the Laughlins, but above that it turns into gravel.

Meadow House is located directly across the road from Robin Hill. You can still see how it was constructed by enlarging a farmhouse that was already there – so I presume – when Aunt Leila acquired the property.

I don't know when Meadow House became the residence of her nephew. For that matter, I don't know anything about the early relationship between Jas and his aunt. I used to infer that since the relationship was so close Jas must have been estranged from his own parents in Pittsburgh, but I no longer make that inference; it is too easy, and certain things I've learned have made it less tenable than it seemed. What I do know is that Jas spent a lot of time at Robin Hill when he was young, and that when he founded New Directions as an undergraduate at Harvard in 1936, Norfolk became the permanent address of the fledgling company. At the very least, Aunt Leila must have been sympathetic to his literary and publishing ambitions. She must have supported him in every way she could. The fact that Jas was extraordinarily dependent on her, emotionally as well as practically, is unmistakable.

To this day she is called Aunt Leila by everyone. I don't remember her married name, and I would need to go into the records to find it. Her husband was called Uncle Dickie, though his name was Lister.

In addition to the mansion, Robin Hill comprised a complex

of other buildings. At a little remove was a tripartite structure consisting of a stable, a carriage house, and a cottage. This was important to New Directions because it became the early headquarters of the company: the stable was turned into an office, the carriage house became a warehouse, and the cottage was the place where early staff members – people like Delmore Schwartz and Kenneth Patchen – lived. Even after the company office was established in New York, the stable remained a workplace and a repository for files and other appurtenances of the business, including a complete stock of New Directions titles from the beginning. In addition, a good-sized barn, always called the Frothingham Barn (I don't know why), was located above the mansion and was converted into a dwelling, and then up a steep hill in the woods nearby was a camp, so-called, which was actually a sturdy and attractive rustic house, inaccessible in winter. Other outbuildings – toolsheds, a greenhouse, a small barn for the sheep – were noticeable, as were vegetable gardens, mowed lawns, pathways, etc. One of the workers on the estate, Leon Deloy, lived in a house at the edge of the property across from the cottage; by the time I came to Norfolk the house had been given to him and he was working at a job somewhere else, I think in Winsted. At the other side of the woods was a small lake called Tobey Pond; part of the shoreline, with a substantial stone lodge and a dock for boating and swimming, belonged to the estate. Robin Hill was, in other words, a bustling enclave at one time in the best manorial tradition, though by the time I saw it Aunt Leila was old and ill, confined to the mansion, and the ambient activity had somewhat subsided.

Jas visited Aunt Leila twice a day during her final illness. He would disappear from Meadow House for a couple of hours and then unobtrusively reappear, and everyone knew where he

Laughlin at the Robin Hill cottage where Hayden Carruth stayed.

Ann and James Laughlin at Meadow House, ca. 1975.

had been – across the road at Robin Hill. He has written about these visits in his "Byways," how the two consoled each other for their hardships, how Aunt Leila sustained her nephew with her wisdom and affection. She must have been an extraordinary person. I wish I had known her.

◇◇◇

When we went skiing together on the trails through the woods that the workers kept cleared, Jas usually went ahead, because he was by far the better skier. But he would stop every once in a while and wait for me to catch up. I would come up to him and find him standing still on his skis.

As we stood there in the snowy woods we were surrounded by profound silence, a wonderful quiet. Jas would look at me without saying anything, and then begin skiing again.

◇◇◇

The task of cataloging his magazines did not take long – three or four days, as I recall – and then I went home. But not long afterward Jas asked me if I'd be willing to move to Norfolk and undertake a considerably bigger job for him. This was an enormous departure for me, of course, but one I felt I was ready for. It scared me, but I knew I had to seize the opportunity. I said yes.

This was in 1960. The job was to renovate and organize the old correspondence files of New Directions from 1936 to the present, preparing them for deposit in the library at Harvard. The files were stored in the stable in eight or ten full-sized filing cabinets. The idea was that I should work in the stable a few hours each day and live in the cottage rent-free; this would be my compensation. I'd still have plenty of time for my own work, and plenty of quiet and solitude in which to do it.

I moved to Norfolk in the spring of 1960, in May or June. The cottage was completely furnished; all I needed to bring with me were my clothes, my typewriter, and a few books – an easy transfer in my little MGA. The cottage was in fact a small but solid and sturdy house, sided with white clapboards; it had a little portico in front, an impressive slate roof, four rooms on the ground floor, an attic above, a full basement below. The front yard, facing the road about fifty yards away, was a huge tangle of rhododendron – in bloom it made the cottage look like a picture postcard – and in back was a small lawn before the edge of the woods. The driveway, beside the cottage and leading behind it to the stable and carriage house, was actually the first part of an unpaved, single-lane road that went through the woods from Mountain Road to Tobey Pond, twisting among stands of spruce and hemlock, crossing a small brook, running beside a bog where pitcher plants and many mosses grew, and ending by the shore of the pond, next to the lodge.

The first morning I was in Norfolk I woke early in my strange bed, feeling half excited by my new adventure and half intimidated by the peculiarity of my situation. My life had been broken several times already; I was thirty-nine years old, and had survived college, the war, two marriages, the insane asylum, the publication of my first book, and years of extreme reclusion; but this seemed the strangest departure of all. I was a poor boy living on an obviously affluent estate, I was a young poet living where first-rate poets had lived before me. Above all, I was a defective – a man completely defeated by the world – who was nevertheless venturing into the world again, however limited that world might be. On the first morning I was up with the sun, dressed and out, nervy, heading down the road to

Tobey Pond for a look at my new surroundings. But before I'd gone a quarter-mile I was attacked by more blackflies and deerflies than I'd ever seen before, buzzing around my head, in my hair, even down my shirt collar and up my sleeves, harrying me as if they were the Eumenides, driving me – running, stumbling, flailing the air around my head – back to the cottage. It was a somewhat discouraging initiation. But at least it demonstrated that even the rich cannot escape our common scourges.

◇◇◇

Aunt Leila died during the brief time between my job with the old magazines in the attic of Meadow House and my return to Norfolk to take up residence in the cottage.

When I arrived Jas was gone. He was out west somewhere, in California apparently. I imagined him seeking consolation for his grief among his friends, people like Kenneth Rexroth and Larry Ferlinghetti. Not until years later, many years, did he confess to me that he had gone off with a woman from one of the neighboring towns in Connecticut. Who she was, I still don't know. He told me her name, but I didn't write it down. He and Ann had been married for a short time at that point; Ann wasn't exactly a bride, but she was a newly married woman. She never indicated to me that she knew what Jas had done, though I'm certain, looking back, that she did. She had been deserted; she was suffering her own grief. Myself, I was so naive that I never suspected, not for an instant. Jas's confession, when it came years later, took me completely by surprise. Yet I knew he had a mistress in New York and several more in Europe. It's true: I was the very image of feckless gullibility.

More will be said about Jas and his women in the succeeding parts of this narrative, of course, but now I must write about

Ann. She was Jas's second wife. I never knew the first, though I saw photographs of her and heard a little about her – not from Jas but from others; she came from Salt Lake City and lived, after she and Jas separated, in Hingham, Massachusetts. Her name was Margaret, she was called Maggie, and she was the mother of Jas's two elder children, Paul and Leila. Ann's family name was Resor, and the Resors were connected in some important way with the J. Walter Thompson advertising agency in New York. In other words, Ann had plenty of money of her own. She told me that she had decided to marry Jas the first time she saw him, which was when he was emerging from an elevator in some office building in New York – she was that smitten. Jas was, as I've said, tall, strong, and I guess good-looking; that is, he didn't seem especially handsome to me, but one can have no doubt, pragmatically speaking, that many women found him essentially irresistible. Ann did not tell me how she conducted her campaign of courtship, but however it was, it worked. She and Jas were married. She became the mistress of Meadow House.

When I arrived in Norfolk the second time, Ann was alone in the house, except for Wonza and the other workers. She kept busy; Ann was a manager, a demon of a manager – she liked nothing better than making plans, making arrangements. In the house, on the grounds, in the town she organized everything. One day she would be directing the groundskeeper in moving a lilac tree, another day she would be in Hartford buying a piece of furniture, or in Great Barrington buying a fine imported shirt. From the moment she had arrived in Norfolk, I think, she had been engaged in local charities, projects for the improvement of the school or library, that sort of thing. She and I spent a good deal of time together during that first summer when Jas was away. She would ask me to have dinner with her at Meadow

House two or three times a week, or to accompany her when she was doing errands in Canaan or Winsted. She talked volubly, obsessively, about Jas. And the main burden of her talk was what she could do to make him more comfortable when he came home.

We would sit in the living room at Meadow House after dinner, facing each other on either side of the hearth or looking out the window at the birch trees in the field, and she would tell me about her newest schemes and worries. Frankly, most of these seemed to me pitiably trivial. She never hinted at the real source of her anxiety, which was not merely Jas's absence but his absence with another woman. Would he prefer a mahogany kneehole desk or a worktable of pine with pigeonholes attached to the wall behind it? Should he have a special desk for working on his stamp collection? Should she build a new garage for his car? Maybe Jas would like to get rid of the sheep now that Aunt Leila was gone? Or perhaps he would like to have the house repainted in another color? Etc., etc. Her appetite for this kind of practical agonizing was insatiable. I listened. I tried to be interested. After all Ann was almost the first person outside my family I'd spent any time with for years, and I was grateful for her friendship, which seemed and was genuine. Indeed some of her scheming was to make *me* more comfortable. She would rearrange the furniture in the cottage, or buy a new appliance for my kitchen. She would ask again and again if there was anything more I needed. She was indefatigable in her managing, which was essentially mothering. If I had been more at ease with myself and the world, I would have resented her directorial endeavors; I think other people definitely would have, but I was too passive to feel anything but gratitude for whatever happened to me. It had to be an improvement over my past.

Ann was tall, a couple of inches taller than I was, which

would have made her about 5'10". She had red hair and a somewhat angular face with a straight nose and a strong jaw. She wasn't a beauty, but she was good-looking, attractive, and had a fine complexion and beautiful hazel eyes, and she dressed casually but elegantly in summer-weight sweaters and skirts. When she was working outdoors she wore khaki dungarees and tied a bandanna around her head. When she went with me in my little sports car she looked perfectly at home and she liked the muttering sound of its softly muffled engine. But usually when we went somewhere together we were in her car, a gray Ford Falcon, and she did the driving. I think she may have felt my MGA was a little vulgar, though she never said so.

In fact, Ann was the epitome of the Radcliffe girl from the 1940s – sensitive, intelligent, liberal, and indelibly aristocratic. But I don't remember where she actually went to school.

Emotionally and temperamentally she was as strong as an ox. And she gave the appearance of happiness and good cheer; a number of people have told me that this was their impression. For my part, however, I always detected, or thought I detected, an element of forcing behind her ebullience. In any group, even in the family, her speech tended to be a little theatrical, with high-pitched bleats of satisfaction or gladness. Fond as I was of her and still am, for she was a loving and warm-hearted friend, I always felt sorry for her too, and pitied her for the hardships she endured and suppressed.

◇◇◇

During the years when I was living at my parents' house I continued to write poems. This wasn't easy. From one point of view, writing is an act of supreme aggression, after all, a demand laid on the world, and consequently for someone like me it was a terribly risky thing to do. I used to say that writing a line of poetry was like squeezing old, half-hardened glue from a tube. It was. Nevertheless I persisted, and my first book was published in 1959, when I was thirty-nine years old, by Macmillan.[10]

With the help of Albert Camus and Jean-Paul Sartre, I had learned lucidity and authenticity. I had even learned recklessness. If you're going to stand me up against the wall for being who I am, go ahead and do it: I'll write my poems anyway.

My second book was a long poem in four parts called *Journey to a Known Place*. I had finished writing it and had sent a copy of it to Jas before I went to Norfolk, and he volunteered to publish it at New Directions. I was pleased, of course. Jas wanted to do it as a limited edition, and he engaged Harry Duncan of Iowa City to do the job. Again I was pleased because I had known and admired Duncan's work at the Cummington Press in Massachusetts where he and Claude Fredericks had been partners. But my pleasure was tempered by knowing that a limited edition would have only a small circulation. Jas countered this by saying that after the book had been out for a while New Directions would publish a cheap edition—"by offset on butcher paper," he said—and send it free to all the names on the mailing list.

For reasons that are indistinct to me now this never happened. The poem was included in one of the New Directions annuals a few years later and then in a book called *For You* in 1970. But the point here is that the limited edition appeared finally during that first summer I spent in Norfolk. It was beautiful; Duncan had done his usual splendid job.[11] As it happened,

10. Thanks to Emile Capouya, a great editor who for a few years consented to work on the staff of the big publishing house. The book was *The Crow & the Heart*.

11. Years later I saw it listed in a bookseller's catalog for $1,000. Once a fellow out west wrote to me, saying he had stolen a copy from the Oklahoma City library and then someone else had stolen it from him. He wanted me to tell him where he could steal another.

the day I received my first copy I opened the package in the post office right away to look at it, and Rose Marie Dorn was there. I showed it to her. Then impulsively I scribbled her name in it and gave it to her. Three months later Rose Marie and I were married.

Rose Marie, who was a refugee from East Germany, worked as a governess in the household of Gabriel and Helen Hauge.[12] Helen was Ann's sister, and that summer the Hauges were occupying the camp on Aunt Leila's estate. They had a big family, five or six kids or maybe more. Rose Marie, who had been a pediatric nurse in Dresden before her escape to the West, was in charge. She was a slight woman, she looked like a girl; she spoke with a soft foreign accent; the children adored her.

When Jas learned that Rose Marie and I were planning to marry, an expression of doubt came over his face. "You won't find much intellectual companionship there, will you?" – or words to that effect. His prejudice slipped out. How could a servant girl be a suitable partner for an educated American poet? But I knew Rose Marie was as smart as anyone. She had memorized reams of German poetry, for instance, when she was doing forced labor in a Communist camp in Saxony, even though her formal education (except for nursing school) had been cut off when she was twelve, by the invading Russian army. Besides, the Silesian peasantry she came from – or any peasantry – were, *in posse*, my favorite people.

◇◇◇

The truth is that that summer of my strange and fearful outventuring was lucky for me beyond what anyone could have

12. Pronounced "Howgee" with a hard "G." Gabriel Hauge was a prominent economist in the banking world of New York and had served as a consultant to President Eisenhower.

considered the remotest possibility. Who would have foreseen that a woman like Rose Marie and a man like me could possibly meet and marry in a place like Norfolk, Connecticut? The idea was patently preposterous. Well, we did, we met and married – thanks to Jas. We occupied the cottage for two years, more or less, and Jas was always courteous and attentive to Rose Marie, though of course a little reserved, as he was toward everyone. When our son was born, David, named after my brother, Ann became his godmother. He was in effect adopted into the Laughlin family, contemporary with the two children who were born to Ann and Jas at about the same time, Robert and Henry.

◇◇◇

At the end of that first summer, in late August or September, Jas came home. He settled quickly into his domestic and professional routine, as if he had never been away. He was a master of modern travel. I knew that, of course; during the years at Intercultural I'd seen him take off for Paris or Bangkok at scarcely more than a moment's notice. Now I saw how expert he was at commuting. He spent three or four days each week in New York, living in the Village apartment, working at the office. He traveled by train from Millerton, New York, which was about half an hour from Norfolk and nearly three hours from Manhattan, and sometimes he asked me to drive him to Millerton or to pick him up there. He always had a fat briefcase with him, really a satchel, stuffed with books and manuscripts, and he worked as comfortably on the train or in the car as he did everywhere else. This was another of his personal accommodations to life in the twentieth century.

Yet he lived in the Renaissance too, in Italy or southern France. With his mistresses, his books by Ovid, Catullus, and

Dante, his taste for good wine, his restlessness, his ease of manner among the famous and powerful – well, he could have traveled quite handsomely on horseback, or grandly in a coach and four. He would have liked that. He actively disliked much of the trappings of modern technological capitalism in America. He disliked telephones, because he thought the written word was both more trustworthy and more elegant than the spoken word. Yet he used phones as frequently and easily as anyone. He called me just a few days before he died, trying to persuade me to take on a particular job of literary hackwork that needed to be done. And I'm sure he made many an impromptu assignation over the phone.

"Hayden," he would say when he called me, using his dry, humorous tone, "I need a favor." Immediately I sat back and waited for some enormous strange request. And when it came I almost always did it.

I remember when he wanted to do a paperback reprint of the translation of Sartre's *La Nausée*, hoping to attract an audience of college students at the time when European Existentialism had become a fad in this country, hoping, in other words, to make a little money for New Directions and at the same time spread the influence of modern European culture in this country. He asked me to do an introduction for the book, a somewhat pedagogical piece aimed toward the students. I had been closely interested in the movement of European thought and feeling that was called Existentialism, and I'd written a book about Albert Camus, whom I admired enormously. It was easy for me to write a few pages about the philosophical issues underlying Sartre's novel and about Sartre's intentions in writing it. I used simple language, and in fact I oversimplified the whole matter, as one inevitably does when one is paraphrasing a work of art. But Jas was delighted with what I'd done. "Hayden," he said, "you're a real pro." And he sent me a check for $100.

The reason Jas liked me – or one of the reasons – was that he had so much trouble with other poets who were vain and touchy when it came to doing ordinary work. I was a poet with a poet's imagination who nevertheless had been trained as a newspaperman, who knew about publishing, who respected the need for plain utilitarian writing in many circumstances, and who didn't feel that he was "selling out" if he produced copy for a book jacket or blurbage for an advertisement. I did these things easily, and I enjoyed doing them. Jas was glad to use my practical talents.

He told me once that the poet he most enjoyed working with was Thomas Merton, in part because Tom was so good at writing jacket copy for his own books.

Another typical job I did for him was typing the manuscript of Pound's anthology, *Confucius to Cummings*. I was a good typist, meticulous. Pound's "manuscript" was a box full of notes, copies, fragments. I arranged it, typed it, put in the right footnotes; I did whatever was needed. I even conferred with Pound a couple of times. I remember Pound complaining about the paucity of American poetry, saying he couldn't find anyone to put in the anthology between Freneau and the mid-nineteenth century. I don't know whom I suggested, perhaps Bryant (whose "Thanatopsis" is a better poem than most people today can admit), but we ended with a piece of satirical light verse by Halleck.

The best part of the anthology was the generous selection of Shakespeare's songs and Pound's notes on them, from which I learned a good deal about Pound. And about myself.

When offset printing became common, so that "typesetting" could be done on a typewriter rather than by Linotype or Monotype, Jas offered to set me up with a fancy typewriter and let me produce camera-ready copy of New Directions books. He thought that because I was a poet, unlike most typists, I could arrange poems on the page as they were supposed to be arranged. He also thought this might be an answer to my poverty, because I was living then in the northern woods on next to nothing. For my part, I liked the idea. I thought I could work comfortably in my little shack next to the brook, and do the job Jas wanted, fitting the work into my routines in the fields and woods and barn. I don't know why this never panned out – perhaps because the people in the office in New York convinced Jas that it wasn't feasible to work with a compositor so far away from the city – but it didn't. I was disappointed. If it had, I might be living yet in the Green Mountains, not exiled to upstate New York.

◇◇◇

A shift of focus here, a shift of the focusing intelligence. I've been writing these remembrances so far in the past tense, but working spontaneously, somewhat randomly, and perhaps it was inevitable that the writing should veer toward the present at some point and turn into a kind of a diary. I'm writing at the end of the winter in 1998; today is March 8. Yesterday I received the news that Gertrude is back in the hospital with an "infection," apparently not specified by the doctors. She is comatose, full of morphine. I spoke with Paul, Jas's son, who has evidently become the family manager and is in Norfolk to take care of Gertrude's taxes. He said that a few days ago they were ready to "pull the plug," but that then Gertrude began to show a small improvement, so they didn't, and now they're waiting to see if she is well enough to die at home instead of in the hospital.

The complex of people and events that precipitated these

remembrances is still ongoing, in other words. Jas died last November (at about the same time when my daughter, Martha, also died). Then in December, out in Seattle, Denise Levertov, who was one of the important figures in the complex, died too. And now Gertrude.

I simply cannot disengage myself from this process of catastrophe, whether or not it is damaging to the compositional strategy of my work.

For some years Gertrude has confided in me. I'm sure in others too. We have carried on a kind of abstract but tender flirtation, two old friends who know what the score is. We have commiserated with one another, she with her lung cancer, I with my emphysema. We have fantasized about our going out together, i.e., side by side, hitched to the same oxygen tank, sharing a bottle of wine. "Maybe we could have a little mild sex before we go," Gertrude said.

Gertrude is rather conventionally religious. She goes to church, says her prayers, has visions of heaven – quite genuinely and vividly. The fact that her envisionings are a little too cherubic for most people's taste doesn't matter to her. I wonder what she is thinking now.

Years ago she was a good-looking young woman, a representative American blonde, but not at all pouty; on the contrary, good-natured and full of fun. Paul can remember her from the old days, before Jas and Ann married; a "pistol," he calls her. For my part, I remember her around the Intercultural office and on the streets of New York, in the bars and restaurants. Always smiling and laughing. Always tagging after Jas. She used to complain to me because he dragged her to so many high-powered cultural events, exhibitions by the New York abstractionists, concerts by the electronic composers. "What a bore," she would whisper and make a face at me behind Jas's back.

I have one of her paintings, a nine-by-twelve watercolor, on the wall of my home. At first glance it seems a conventional flower painting, a blue translucent vase with a bouquet of pink carnations, very well done. But then you notice that goldfish are swimming in the water inside the vase. You see that the whole thing is set on the middle of the ocean and that little elephants are swimming, diving, cavorting in the waves. It is a perfect work of whimsy. Not very fashionable in our time, the cognoscenti in New York would scorn it, I'm sure. But it is brilliantly executed, and full of the gentleness and sweetness of Gertrude.

She had to give up painting a couple of years ago when her vision began to fade because of macular degeneration. She complained. She complained volubly and unrestrainedly. She liked to use gutter language, at least with me. "This is so shitty, Hayden," she would say.

The last time I spoke with her on the phone, about a week ago, she was using oxygen and she said it made her feel much better. Moreover, the doctor had told her that her recent chest X rays were "clear." She sounded strong. She said she wanted to see me and tell me some things she knew about Jas, especially about his "womanizing." I wish I had jumped in the car and driven the 200 miles to Norfolk immediately, but I didn't – in the circumstances such a trip was too much for me. Shitty, indeed.

◇◇◇

My job in Norfolk was simple enough if somewhat tedious, somewhat dusty. Sneezing and snuffling, I went through the files in the stable from A to Z, thousands and thousands of documents, mostly correspondence but other things too. I read everything. I put all the papers into what I thought was good order, arranging the dated documents chronologically, fitting in undated documents where I thought they reasonably might go. I smoothed out those that had been folded or crumpled. I mended torn papers with transparent tape. I made sure that everything fitted snugly and neatly in the file folders and that the folders were properly labeled. I refiled papers that had been originally misfiled. What else? I don't remember. I was following instructions, trying to prepare the files for shipment to the archives at some university.

Did I realize that this was "made-work" – unnecessary, contrived for my benefit? Did I know then, as I do now, that when the files reached the archives some graduate student in librarianship would be assigned to do the same work all over again? Again, I don't remember. I may have suspected as much, but I don't think so. As I've said, I was extraordinarily naive, and if someone whose knowledge far exceeded mine, someone like Jas, told me to do something, I assumed it had to be done. But as I look back now, I don't believe those files were ever deposited in an academic library; I think they may still be at Meadow House, in the vault that Jas later constructed at one end of the house, in which to preserve the papers for himself and for the many visiting scholars who ask to use them.

What I think now is that Jas and my doctor, Peter Laderman, were in cahoots.[13] At some point Jas had looked up Peter and asked him if he – Jas – could be of help. When Peter felt that I was ready to take a step away from home and in the direction of a normal life, he told Jas, and Jas manufactured the work for me in Norfolk. It was a remarkable manipulation, if that's what it was, and it was successful. That step was a small step, but it really was in the right direction, and thirty years later I was almost living in the real world again.

13. But when I've asked Peter about this he denies it and says he has never had any connection with Laughlin. I leave what I've written as is, however, because it represents my feeling.

But I had no inkling at the time that any such scheme was in effect.[14] Only years later did my suspicion become aroused. And then, owing to the nature of our friendship, I never felt able to ask Jas point blank if my suspicions were correct. I think in letters, years later, I may have hinted at the question once or twice, and I think Jas simply ignored my hesitant intimations, or pretended not to understand them.

I heard little from Jas during that first summer, an occasional note posted from California but nothing else. At summer's end he came back to Norfolk, inspected what I had done, and pronounced it okay, though I don't remember when I actually finished the work. I do remember that as soon as I was through with the files, Jas came up with other jobs for me. During the time I was in Norfolk, I worked on the manuscript of Pound's anthology, *Confucius to Cummings,* typing and cutting and pasting, I wrote the notes that were appended to the back of Raja Rao's novel, *Kanthapura,* working from answers that Rao recorded on tape to my written questions, I worked with Jas on the *New Directions Reader,* though in fact I did most of the work and made most of the choices, I wrote my abortive history of the publishing company, I worked on the last-minute manuscript of Tennessee Williams's *Night of the Iguana,* inserting the revisions that Williams phoned to me from rehearsals and tryouts in Philadelphia – for purposes of copyright the play had to be published on the night of its opening performance, and Williams preferred to have New Directions publish both the trade and acting editions of his work, rather than relying on one of the theatrical publishers – I did a good many small jobs such as writing blurbs and catalog copy, etc. But I was never on the staff or payroll of New Directions. I can't remember if Jas paid

14. And I don't mean to suggest that the work I did for Jas wasn't always in some way useful. Anyone who has worked in a publishing office knows that endless clerical chores need doing and that no one wants to do them. Somebody has to.

me for what I did out of his own pocket. In fact I have no memory at all of what I did for cash during the two years I lived in Norfolk, and perhaps that is significant – though I'm sick of psychoanalyzing myself. But I know I didn't lack. Rose Marie and I went shopping for groceries every week in Canaan. We paid our hospital bill when our son was born. We had gas for our car – after we married I turned in my MGA and bought a SAAB, one of the earliest SAABs imported to the U.S., and then at some point I also bought a beautiful thirdhand MGTD for $600 from a fellow over near Manchester, and Rose Marie and I went touring around Norfolk in it with our boy, the Bo, in a little jump seat I rigged for him in the back.

My work for Jas always left me plenty of time for myself. I went walking every day, exploring the woods, going up Canaan Mountain to the reservoir and Seldom Seen Pond and the Yale tree plantation, and sometimes I wrote poems. At the end of the first summer I had a small book, which I called *The Norfolk Poems* and dedicated to Ann and Jas. It was published eventually, though while I was still in Norfolk, by Carroll Coleman at The Prairie Press in Iowa City. I had admired Carroll's work ever since I had seen my friend Jim Cunningham's book called *The Judge Is Fury*, which Carroll had designed and produced for Alan Swallow of Denver – a very beautiful book – and I simply sent the manuscript of *The Norfolk Poems* to Carroll without any prior introduction. Or perhaps we had already been in touch about something else, I don't remember. Carroll did his usual good work – not as spectacular as Cunningham's book, but workmanlike and attractive – and he published and sold the book under his own imprint. When I received my copies, I immediately took one up to Meadow House and gave it to Jas. He lay on the sofa in the living room next to the fireplace – sprawled out at full length, which was impressive – and read it through.

Then he got up and said, "A lot of good stuff in there, Hayden."

Naturally, I felt let down. It wasn't until later that I found out this was high praise from Jas. He never expressed himself really enthusiastically about the work of any contemporary, as far as I know. This was part of his prudence, the same prudence that permitted him to run New Directions for sixty years on the brink of financial disintegration without ever abandoning it.

I've said that my work on the old files was somewhat tedious. It was. But it was somewhat exciting too. What could be better than reading years and years of correspondence from Pound and Williams, from Dylan Thomas and Pablo Neruda, from hundreds of writers whom I had admired all my life. Some letters were particularly affecting: the late letters from William Carlos Williams, for instance, written after his stroke. They were done on a typewriter, and they would begin

Dear dear dear dear dear dear dear dear dear

and would be followed by a line or two of similarly aphasic language. The top of the page would be wrinkled where Williams had grabbed it and torn it out of the typewriter carriage. Then at the bottom the letter would be finished in Floss's handwriting. It was heartbreaking – all that marvelous volubility reduced to a garble. It was also puzzling. I could vaguely understand the mechanism of aphasia in spoken language, but on a typewriter? No, you can see as well as hear what you're doing on a typed page, you can at least go back and X out your mistakes. But there it was, aphasia spelled out in literal transcription. Years later when I was camping in Yosemite I met a young doctor from San Francisco who had been a friend of Williams's, actually a medical protégé back in New Jersey, and he squatted in the campground and drew a diagram of the brain in the dust

Laughlin and Ezra Pound in Italy, ca. 1935.

Laughlin in his New Directions
office in New York City.

Ezra Pound and Laughlin on a
walk in Rapallo, 1965.

with a stick, and showed me how the centers governing spoken and written language are next to each other and connected. The stroke that had disabled Williams had wrecked all four of the language-controlling sectors: those for writing and speaking, those for reading and hearing.

I also discovered in the files what vile egomaniacs some writers can be, people who heaped contumely on Jas's head and on anyone else's head on the staff of New Directions, people like Kenneth Rexroth, Djuna Barnes, Vladimir Nabokov. I'd had a little of this myself in my editorial days in Chicago and New York; but never anything to compare with what I found in those files. It was revealing. Jas was supporting these people in every way he could, personally and professionally; he was paying their rent, bailing them out of jail, promoting their reputations assiduously; and in spite of these vitriolic attacks on him his efforts never wavered. Then and now I've taken this as a measure of his devotion to literature, so genuine and stalwart.

◇◇◇

I met Williams only once in my life. It was in Chicago when I was on the staff of *Poetry*, but I think before I became editor. Williams was taking his first trip after his first stroke. Ted Roethke – or someone in Seattle – had persuaded him to give a reading at the University of Washington, and for some reason Williams had not only agreed to do it but had climbed on the train in New York alone, i.e., without Floss. In those days everyone who traveled across country by train – few were using planes then – had to lay over at Union Station in Chicago for eight hours in order to make connections, and everyone, or nearly everyone, who was a poet put in a call to the *Poetry* office. Usually these visits were impromptu, but Williams had let us know ahead of time that he was coming. We picked him up at the station and brought him back to 232 East Erie. He looked awful. He was haggard and frail. He was obviously scared to death. He said something about the folly of traveling without Floss, though I can't quote him exactly, and we asked him if he needed to see a doctor. He said no.

In those days we kept a bottle of Old Guckenheimer's[15] in the bottom drawer of the filing cabinet in the main office. We offered Williams a drink, which he accepted. In no time he was looking much better and talking a blue streak. His head was full of anecdotes of artistic life in the twenties and thirties, all his friends from Greenwich Village. He went on at length about Mina Loy, I remember, and he was not only articulate, as one would expect, but very spontaneous and enthusiastic.

The plan was to have lunch at Marion Stroebel's big handsome apartment on the North Side. We went there. We sat at a large round dining table with a damask cloth over it and lots of gleaming silverware and crystal. Wine was served. An immense tureen of oyster stew was set on the table. We began to drink and eat, but Williams kept talking – and talking and talking and talking. His gum began to bleed, the upper front gum. Blood sprayed from his mouth all over the beautiful white tablecloth, a crimson mist, but Williams couldn't stop – or wouldn't. He dabbed at his mouth with his napkin, and kept eating and talking and spattering. Marion, bless her heart, flinched a little, I think, but made no protest. And Williams would accept no help.

That's what I remember, with amusement and affection: the great man sitting there at the table of the rich spewing blood all over it and talking about Cummings and Edna Millay.

Other friends of mine – Denise Levertov, Allen Ginsberg – knew Williams well and told me about their visits to his home in

15. The cheapest blended whiskey.

Rutherford. But none knew him as well as Jas. You could tell by the letters that they were close and trusting in their relationship, and that Jas regarded Williams as both a friend and a mentor. Jas himself has written about this; see his *Byways* and his prose fiction. Then for a while a rift occurred. One of the subeditors Jas had hired at New Directions turned out to be a nefarious self-seeker, who not only left New Directions and went to Random House – Jas would never have objected to this – but persuaded Williams to go with him. For once Jas became genuinely, overtly angry. He felt that after all he had done, publishing Williams's work for years and keeping it in print, poetry, fiction, essays, including the wonderful *Collected Poems* of 1939, which was my first introduction to the great man's writing – Jas felt that after all this, Williams had betrayed him. The migration to Random House was a gross disloyalty. For a while their friendship became acrimonious, and I believe lawyers were involved on both sides. But finally Williams recognized his error and apologized for it and they became good friends again. They remained so until Williams died, and then Jas continued to visit Floss in Rutherford whenever he could.

Jas was not unsentimental. However rigorously he ruled out displays of sentiment in his own behavior – and he was rigorous indeed – his feelings were strong and, if you knew him well enough, unmistakable. He never said much to me about our friendship; an observer might have thought it didn't exist. Jas always ended his letters, for instance, with "As ever" or, if I had been complaining, with "Chin up" – no affectionate farewells. But once – I think the last time I visited Meadow House in June or July of 1997 – he held my hand in both of his while I was leaving, and gripped my shoulder. I don't remember what he said exactly, but tears were in his eyes and his voice was shaky. He knew his end was near.

◇◇◇

Impossible to think of Meadow House without remembering the sheep – seeing them, hearing them, smelling them. Except in the worst winter weather they were always there in the meadow, grazing picturesquely beneath the little grove of white birches. Sometimes they would develop an instantaneous panic and go thundering off full tilt to another part of the meadow or around the back of the house to the barn. The pounding of little hooves. The chorus of sheepish voices. Sometimes, especially when they were newly shorn, their bawling would be loud, continuous, and annoying.

Jas called them the Gabriel Heaters, in allusion to a political commentator who had a regular program on the radio in those days and spoke with a gravelly voice.

Occasionally for lunch at Meadow House we'd have little loin chops, prepared beautifully by Wonza, garnished with mint and savory – a very fine lunch. Jas would point out, with self-mocking satisfaction, that the meal came from his own estate.[16]

◇◇◇

When Jas was asked to designate his occupation, he would put down "investor." He seemed to think – or to conclude instinctively – that he would breach the limits of immodesty or presumption if he called himself a publisher. Even worse would have been to call himself a writer or a poet. Yet publishing, editing, writing were what he did; he was preeminently a literary person. No one who knew him could be mistaken about the direction in which his primary energy and attention were aimed.

16. However, his daughter Leila has told me that the sheep at Meadow House were inedible and their meat was never served in the dining room. Take your pick.

Why was he hesitant to admit it? Certainly this wasn't an anti-artistic or anti-intellectual bias in himself – far from it. I suspect it was more an imputed anti-intellectualism in others, in his family or among his childhood friends and associates in Pittsburgh. He was sensitive to this. And the truth is that it may not even have existed, or at least not in any significant degree. Yet Jas intuitively hid himself behind such little, halfhearted, nominal gestures, which he knew were useless fictions. Not only that, he knew that everyone else knew it too.

In his early years he wrote a fair number of poems under the name of Hiram Handspring. His Doppelgänger. And of course he loved to write in schoolboy French or in what he called "ski German," which was the language of the international ski resorts in Austria and Switzerland, a kind of koine. Disguise was part of his natural personality. Along with it, corollary to it, was a need to compartmentalize his life extremely, to keep one hand from knowing what the other hand was doing. Which meant that his friends and associates often did not know what he was doing with other friends and associates, or even that the others existed.

Was he an investor? Yes. How much time and effort did he give to it? I don't know, I had only glimpses of it, but the glimpses were enough to tell me that he was serious about it, serious and professional. In a sense he was quite right to call himself an investor. That's how he "made his living." He told me once that his father – or possibly his grandfather – had given him $100,000 when he was an undergraduate at Harvard, circa 1936, and had told him that that's all he'd get from the family until he received his inheritance. He used the $100,000 to pay his own expenses and to underwrite the beginning of New Directions, though Aunt Leila helped too. But the important thing is that he also invested part of this money, and by the time his inheritance came to him, twenty or more years later, he was already a rich man in his own right – at least that's what he led me to believe. And I do believe it. Granted, $100,000 in 1935 was probably a million or more in terms of 1998. He still did pretty well.

Once when I was working on the New Directions files I came across a document that shouldn't have been there. It was an order from Jas to his stockbroker to sell all his remaining stock in the Jones & Laughlin Steel Corporation. Naturally it set me to wondering. I was certain the decision to bail out of the family business had been a hardheaded, practical decision, because, in 1950 or so, Jas could foresee that the steel business in this country was declining. But at the same time, divesting himself of his stock in the corporation that had established the Laughlin fortune must have been something of a wrench. A hell of a wrench. Was it a wrench of pleasure or a wrench of regret? Probably both.

Years later on another occasion I was at dinner with the Laughlins in Meadow House, and one of the other guests, a woman, was a financial person, a specialist of some kind. She sat at Jas's right hand, and he devoted himself almost exclusively to her during the whole dinner while the rest of us talked about something else. At one point she said, "What's the good of having two million dollars in CDs when you can put it in something that will bring a better return?" Her question jumped out at me and stuck in my mind, I suppose partly because I could understand it (whereas much of the rest of their conversation was beyond me) and partly because the sum of money was so enormous. It was another little glimpse, a little window separating my world from theirs. Being at that dinner table was like overhearing the discourse of the gods on Olympus – or perhaps of the fiends at the bottom of hell.

Normally Jas kept his private papers in a room at the back of

Meadow House, a room in the apartment originally reserved for servants. He had a safe back there, a big one. It contained not only his financial papers but the manuscripts of his own writing. I suppose it contained all kinds of things. It was his private cubbyhole, and I doubt that anyone else, even his wife, had access to it, though probably he had given the combination to his lawyer for use in case of emergency.

As I've said before, Jas did his work in the living room at Meadow House, meaning his editorial and other professional work, and he also wrote or dictated personal letters at the desk there, and worked on his stamp collection. The office at the back of the house was where he wrote his poems. I was never invited back there, though I knew he had many manuscripts, both poetry and prose, stored in that safe. A couple of times he hinted to me about the stuff in that safe, accounts of his relationships with Pound and Williams, for instance, as well as his poems, and I itched to look at them. At that time I never did. Mostly, however, he was at the desk in the living room when he was at home at all and not in New York or on the golf course or fishing. It's interesting to note that as he grew older, as he concentrated his attention more and more on his own work, he gradually shifted his primary locus from the living room to the back of the house, until finally the desk in the living room disappeared altogether and was replaced by a table which Ann used as a dining table during her last illness, while she could still sit in her wheelchair, and at which Gertrude later did her painting. The room in the back was just off the kitchen. It overlooked the patio and the meadow. It contained a long table, like a trestle table, and Jas worked at one end of it where he had a kind of podium for his old portable typewriter, so that it was elevated somewhat and slanted toward him: he found this a help in typing with shaky fingers. The door to the kitchen was always open now, and anyone could go into his workspace who wanted to. Jas himself spent more and more time in the kitchen. He and Gertrude often took their meals at the kitchen table next to a big window which looked out on a bird feeder, with part of a flower garden and the woods in the background. Quite a far cry from the day of finger bowls and candles during Ann's regime.

But back to his investing. It takes luck as well as intelligence. Because Jas was a skier and because his first wife, Margaret, came from Salt Lake City, he had done some rough-and-ready cross-country skiing in the Wasatch Mountains, east of the city. The snow was great, the conditions were usually splendid – sunny and dry – and of course the landscape was spectacular. Jas made friends with the mountaineers he used for guides, and then he bought a section of land that came on the market. He put his ski buddies to work at developing it. I've only the vaguest idea of what they did, and I know the operation was often impeded by broken-down lifts, troubles with the government, hindrances of all kinds. But that piece of the Wasatch Range became Alta, one of the most popular skiing resorts in the west, just at the time – after World War II – when Alpine skiing began to catch the public fancy as a sport for everyone. The return on the original investment was considerable, not to say enormous.

◇◇◇

Another person who was at that dinner table with the financial expert, circa 1980, was Paul. During dinner Jas said things that made me cringe. E.g., "Poor Paul, he has no head for this kind of thing," or "Well, I gave Paul my stamp collection, which was worth thousands, and he never did anything with it." Paul said nothing. After dinner Paul and I were standing in the foyer, and he muttered to me, something I didn't catch, but of course I knew what it was.

Laughlin with Masa and Gary Snyder at Kitkitdizze.

Laughlin in the wilds on a trip
with Kenneth Rexroth.

Laughlin at his Alta, Utah,
resort, 1939.

I never understood, and still don't, why Jas disliked his son so much. It was unnatural. But it was apparent and undeniable, no matter how you tried to diminish it.

◇◇◇

During that first summer in Norfolk both Paul and Leila were in evidence at Meadow House, two extremely intelligent and good-looking youngsters, probably sixteen and fifteen years old. I came to know Paul better than Leila, perhaps because she was around less often. Both of them spent a good deal of time with their mother in eastern Massachusetts, which was doubtless a livelier place to be than the lower Berkshires. Leila had dark hair, bright eyes, a beautiful open expression; she was sexy-looking, like any healthy adolescent girl. I remember her dressed in cutoff jeans with a big red patch in the shape of a heart sewn onto the rear. Both Paul and Leila had lived in Norfolk when they were growing up, of course, before their mother and Jas parted company, and everyone in town knew them, liked them. They had many friends their own age, some of whom were present frequently at Meadow House. They went to parties. They went to one party, which was apparently an annual event, that appalled me, a soiree at the field house for the purpose of killing bats. This was done with tennis racquets and squash racquets. I wasn't there, but I envisioned a big dim open space indoors with maimed bats flopping and flapping all around. This was considered great entertainment by the young people.

At that time I was beginning to become seriously interested in motor sports. Not that I ever competed; I didn't have enough money, for one thing, and of course I was too shy. But I did teach myself to drive my MGA efficiently, safely, and fast. (Late one night on the Mass Pike I got it up to 112 mph, which was foolish and dangerous in a little car that hadn't been meticulously balanced. The car was shaking like a leaf.) A couple of times I took Paul with me to the scca races at Lime Rock, which was not far away in Lakeville, and Paul became interested too. The next summer I saw more of him. He bought an MGB and learned how to maintain it and service it himself. We spent many hours talking about automotive topics, which, as all buffs know, are endless. That's one of the agreeable things about a car: it has as many parts as a horse – a great many – but they are easier to understand and one can take care of them oneself.

Paul and I became good friends. After Rose Marie and I moved to Vermont, following our two years in the cottage, Paul came to visit us often, and once he and a friend named Dana spent most of a summer with us, made a garden, experimented with cheese making and cider making, helped me with my chores – everything from cleaning out the henhouse to fixing the water siphon from the spring. Eventually Paul bought a tract of perhaps 100 acres above us on the brook road and turned part of it into a Christmas tree plantation. I think he envisioned building a house there and living near to me. But then he married – a fine girl named Marian – and went to live permanently in Ann Arbor, where he and she had both gone to school. Paul became an Arabic scholar and a collector and broker of important photographic prints and negatives. He was a fine photographer himself, adept in the dark room, and some of the photos I cherish most were taken by him during the time when I lived in Vermont. Then finally I moved away to upstate New York. In recent years we haven't seen each other or had any connection – until the phone call about Gertrude.

Although the news about Gertrude was awful, it was good to talk with him.

Jas could be extraordinarily hard on his children. He could

neglect them without a qualm if he felt like going off on his own for a while – to California or, for that matter, to Sri Lanka. He could neglect them at home too, leaving their care entirely to a succession of governesses. As I've said, he had four children, Paul and Leila with his first wife, then Robert and Henry with Ann. Robert and Henry were born while I was in Norfolk, or not long before, so I saw them when they were small, saw them being trucked here and there by one governess or another, at least one of whom was definitely unsuitable for the job, as I witnessed with my own eyes and ears more than once. A horrible woman. But I never saw the children at the dinner table. Jas and Ann apparently agreed that children were unpleasant – necessary but a nuisance.

Paul was pretty well alienated from his father and had only a somewhat remote connection with Ann. Leila was less affected; she and Jas remained on good terms most of the time, I think. Robert committed suicide when he was in his twenties, living and working as an aspirant film person in California. Henry, the youngest, I've seen only once as an adult, a few years ago when he and I were visiting Meadow House at the same time. He seemed cheerful, smart, friendly, and altogether together, obviously concerned about his father's failing health and wanting to do what he could to be helpful.

◇◇◇

Why was Jas so hard on Paul? Was it that he could not express affection and therefore chose, instinctively, the opposite course? Was he actually proud of his good-looking, capable son, but knew – as he knew the grass was green – that it would be indecorous or humiliating or too self-revealing to say so? At times I thought the case was of this order, but bigger, bigger by far, and more complicated. Ultimately, an enigma.

For my part, having been through years of therapy and analysis, I believe no one can be reduced to – or by – a formula. The attempt is very common, of course, and very degrading to everyone.

◇◇◇

When that first summer ended, the Hauges went home to New York and Rose Marie went with them. But as soon as the children were settled into their schools she quit her job, and we – she and I – became busy. It was a lovely autumn. The famous New England foliage was spectacular, the fine weather lasted a long time. We were married in October and set up housekeeping together in the cottage, surrounded by the woods and flowers, which was exactly what Rose Marie, with her sentimental, baroque Middle-European background, wanted. So did I. Jas was at home now, i.e., when he wasn't in New York or somewhere else – his base was at home. And when the snow came he set out to teach me to ski.

I'd never been on skis in my life. When I was a boy, and then in college, skiing was an aristocratic sport, along with tennis and golf, not for the children of the working class. So I was forty when I first put my feet into a pair of Leila's cross-country boots and strapped on her skis. Jas showed me what to do, the basics, how to glide, climb, stem and snowplow, how to use the poles. He initiated me into the mysteries of waxing, how to gauge temperature, snow quality, atmospheric conditions, etc., in order to choose the right wax, though as far as I could see it remained a mystery and you had to be lucky to hit it right.

When and where Jas learned to ski I don't know for sure, but I expect it was early and in Europe. I do know he attended a

James Laughlin at his Meadow House study.

Hayden Carruth at his Vermont cowshed study, 1964.

secondary school in Switzerland for a while. That's where he learned French and his smattering of German, just as he learned Greek and Latin at Choate. He has written somewhere about memorizing reams of nineteenth-century French poetry at the Swiss school. At any rate, by the time he got to Harvard he was a skier. He visited the ski resorts of New Hampshire and Vermont as often as he could. For a while when he was an undergraduate he skied competitively, until he hurt his back in an accident on the lower slopes of Mount Washington. After college he continued to ski. He was enthusiastic and serious about it, and he began writing articles for the skiing press, an avocation that took him, expenses paid, to most of the well-known ski resorts of the world. He pioneered in cross-country skiing before more than a few people outside of Scandinavia were doing it, and wrote pieces about traversing long mountainous itineraries in virgin snow, staying overnight in improvised shelters, using local guides, both in the Alps and in North America.

I knew this, and I wasn't surprised to find the back entryway at Meadow House full of skiing equipment, the woods all around intersected by ski trails. Some of these were old logging roads or other traces that had been there for a long time, but others were new trails which Jas himself had cut; and he did his share of work in maintaining them, keeping them open in the summer.

That's where he took me to teach me the sport.

I was dubious at first. Who wouldn't be? Soon, however, I took to it with a certain excitement, partly because I found I could actually do it, partly because I discovered it was better exercise than I had anticipated – you could work up a sweat in the coldest weather, and I liked that – but chiefly because two men engaged in a common activity in the woods is such a wondrous blessing in the midst of human struggle and pain. We didn't talk much. When I fell, I cursed. When I did something wrong, Jas told me and showed me how to do it correctly. I never became a good skier, and my attempts at downhill skiing with the big skis and cast-iron boots were dismal. Nevertheless, I learned to navigate in the woods pretty handily. The truth is that you can't talk much when you're skiing, but only when you stop to rest.

I'm reminded of another time, much later, when I was in Saratoga Springs, a guest at Yaddo, the artists' colony there. It was winter. John Cheever was a fellow guest. He had damaged his knee in a downhill accident, and he asked me to show him how to do cross-country skiing, because he had seen me loading skis into my car one afternoon. We went to the golf course. Trails had been made there with one of those mechanical gadgets that cut two parallel tracks through the snow, and we could ski fourteen miles, we estimated, without crossing the same ground. John took to it. He fell sometimes and he was slow, but if I turned back to help him he would wave me away and holler, "Go on, go on, don't pay any attention to me." One part of the trail led through a plantation of half-grown Christmas trees next to the golf course, a place that John particularly liked. The Elysian Fields, he called it. He relished getting away from the pretentious artistic atmosphere of Yaddo. On the way back to Yaddo, we always stopped at a little grocery store at the Five Corners where John bought a box of crackers. "Gots to have my crackers," he said.

Jas and I went skiing every day that winter when he was at home, and when he was away I went skiing by myself. I learned about powder and drifts, corn snow in the spring, how to crouch down low when snow was falling – to increase visibility and reduce the danger of injury when you ran into a tree. We would go up to the top of the "mountain" and ski down one of the roads, or head off through the woods and down the steep hill to the Blackberry River and the low fields by the inn. We would ski across Tobey Pond where a deep cover of unblemished snow lay on the ice, going with a long swinging motion like skaters with outsized skates. We would bushwhack through the dense woods where no track existed, Jas leading the way expertly: he was great at heading full speed into a stand of ash or beech and finding a way through without falling. He would laugh and chortle to himself, and on the other side he would stand and blow his nose and light his pipe. We were both pipe smokers. Like all that tribe, we kept our pipes in our mouths most of the time, no matter what we were doing.

The second winter of my sojourn in Norfolk we did the same thing. Only better.

◇◇◇

Once when I went to Norfolk – it was sometime during the 1970s – I found Jas in the woods. He was down in the bed of the brook where the little road to Tobey Pond passed over a makeshift wooden bridge. He was wearing rubber boots, dungarees, and an old plaid shirt, and he was sweaty and mud-streaked.

What he was doing was building a little "terrace" beside the brook, a small platform, made by lashing together spruce poles he had cut in the woods and laying them flat; then he shored them up with rocks and placed sod on top of them.

He looked up and said, "The value of this job, Hayden, is that it has no value."

He was right. I don't know how much thought he had given to it beforehand, but he had chosen something to do that was absolutely without purpose. No one would ever use that "terrace" by the brook, even assuming that it survived the first spring freshet, which it wouldn't. It was as if Jas had intentionally cast about for a safe domestic outlet into which he could channel some of his enormous energy. He invented a perfectly useless task.

Or did he want to leave a little private mark on the face of the woods? I can understand that. I used to write messages on the undersides of shelf fungi I found growing on trees in the woods – in Norfolk, at Saratoga, in Vermont – messages that no one could ever see who didn't already know they were there.

Sometimes you find in the woods an old shoe or a length of rusty barbed wire still stapled to a tree, and all at once it becomes an object of great beauty and pathos.

Jas was doing a useless job, performing a labor of luxury, which is one of the advantages of life among the well-to-do. There are others. For instance, when the ice and wind of winter knock down two or three slates from your roof, don't worry. Each spring a guy from Torrington comes to replace them. He brings a supply of new slates and a portable spring-press with which to punch holes in them.

◇◇◇

Jas was a smoker. He had been a smoker all his adult life. He smoked a pipe continually and two or three cigars a day. His pipe tobacco was mixed to his own formula by Dunhill's in New York and sent to him in monthly packets; it was an English blend – Virginia and Turkish for the base, some Latakia, perhaps some Macedonian Kavala, perhaps Cavendish and a touch of perique. His cigars were Havana double coronas, claro with candela or English market wrappers, and were also sent to him from Dunhill's.[17] Jas smoked with dedication, in other words, and so did I. The difference was that I also smoked cigarettes

17. In the days before the embargo, of course.

and had smoked them ever since I was a child. I presume Jas had experimented with cigarettes, too; not to have done so at that time would have been very unusual. But I never saw him with a cigarette.

After Rose Marie and I were married I quit smoking cigarettes. I became a full-fledged pipe smoker who smoked twenty pipes a day – and suffered the consequent charring in my mouth – and who enjoyed an occasional cigar when I could afford it. I kept this up for twenty years. It was Rose Marie's doing. She felt that the pipe was better for me than cigarettes because I didn't inhale the pipe smoke into my lungs. But if Rose Marie provided the impetus, Jas provided the model. He was the one who demonstrated that it was possible to get along without cigarettes, even when you were writing.

But what about my father? He had been a lifelong pipe smoker too. And he had died not long before I first went to Norfolk. And he was a reserved, not to say dangerously inhibited, person – like Jas.

Jas was seven years older than I.

Shall I leave it to some kind soul to tell me the significance of all this?[18]

At any rate, the immediate point is that tobacco was an important and serious consideration in our lives, which will seem silly to many people or even outrageous. But many smokers of our generation will understand.

In old age Jas switched to cigars entirely. He even began buying them at the Norfolk Pharmacy instead of relying on a fancy tobacconist in the city. It was part of his general accession to ordinariness which was noticeable in his seventies and eighties. Besides, he became too shaky to handle his pipe competently.

18. Eventually, during a visit to Yaddo, I became rehooked on cigarettes.

Finally, a few months before he died, he yielded to his doctor's command that he give up smoking altogether. He used to write me plaintive little notes to tell me how many days he had gone without a cigar.

◇◇◇

What had originally recommended Norfolk to people of affluence is hard to say. It's a good enough small town in the conventional mode of New England, with a green, a white church and a cemetery, farms, a river, lakes and ponds, hills and valleys, but not essentially different from most other villages in northwestern Connecticut. The town where I grew up, Woodbury, which is thirty miles or so south of Norfolk, was similar topographically, but in the twenties and early thirties, when I lived there, it was a semi-impoverished agricultural community with no rich people at all.[19] In fact a good many refugees from World War I and its aftermath, especially Lithuanians, had settled there and were living on the poorest, stoniest, grubbiest farms imaginable. Nothing like that in Norfolk. I don't know when it was – probably in the last part of the nineteenth century and the first part of the twentieth – but Norfolk had been discovered by rich people who in turn had attracted their own kind, and they had taken over the town.

You couldn't mistake this when I was there. The village itself was clean and attractive without being ostentatiously "restored" or "gentrified," like Lewisburg, Pennsylvania, for instance. More to the point, it was surrounded by the estates of wealthy families – big houses, beautifully kept lawns and gardens, well-preserved woodlands, fields with white fences and horses in them (not cows), etc. The social tone of the place was unmis-

19. Since then Woodbury has become rather posh with paved roads and restored farmhouses. When I drive through it now I can scarcely recognize it.

takable. The local people, remaining descendants of the original farmers, were the shopkeepers, caretakers, housemaids; they were the ones who kept the town going. I don't say they went around all the time tugging their forelocks, but when it came to relations with the rich and powerful they were very damned careful. My neighbor, Leon Deloy, for instance, had a dog, a well-behaved springer spaniel, which somehow got lost and dug a hole in the garden attached to a mansion three-quarters of a mile away. The people complained. Immediately Leon shot the dog.

One of the local institutions that you heard about when I was in Norfolk was the Dolittle Club, named after a lake on the north side of town. I was told by a clerk in the drugstore that you had to be a millionaire to belong to it, which may or may not have been true, but clearly the club had one primary function: to buy up any land that came on the market and prevent newcomers from settling in the town, especially newcomers who might engage in land development or other unseemly commercial activities. I don't think Jas belonged to the Dolittles, but naturally he knew those people, and when Ann came to Norfolk she quickly got to know them too. Both of them belonged to the country club where they played golf together frequently in summer. I expect they played in foursomes with other members of the élite.

Jas introduced me to some of these people, and also to the people who worked in the village at the drugstore, the post office, the library. Norfolk had a very fine small grocery store and a good hardware store. No clothing store, no gift shop or antique gallery, no boutiques. You went to Canaan or Winsted when you wanted to buy a pair of boots. The library was the best I've ever known in a small town.[20] It had an excellent basic

20. The population of Norfolk in 1960 was no more than 1,000 or 1,500 people.

collection, a big comfortable reading room, many newspapers and magazines, and the staff was as intelligent and helpful as any you could hope to meet. They went out of their way to turn up books I needed in my work, getting them from Hartford or New Haven or one of the universities. I don't remember if the library was privately endowed or supported by taxes, but it doesn't matter; in either case the Norfolk gentry knew a good town needed a good library, so they supported theirs generously, whether or not any of them ever used it.

The green in Norfolk, at the top of the main street across from the library, was triangular, what old-time New Englanders called a "heater piece," with shade trees, a lawn, benches, and a large, ornate, decidedly priapic fountain. The main street was Route 44, a secondary road running from New York State to Hartford, and on the other side of it from the center of the village was a huge estate behind a substantial brick wall, owned by two families, the Battells and the Stoeckels. This was used, and still is, by Yale University for its summer school of the arts.

You get the picture. An affluent, good-looking small town with an academic connection. An inn with a good dining room at the edge of town. All within easy distance of the Berkshires – Tanglewood, Jacob's Pillow, and other cultural amenities.

Sometimes Meadow House would become a festive scene. Many cars parked around the circle in front. Lights blazing at all the windows. Ann would be having a dinner party, quite elaborate, cocktails beforehand and cognac and coffee afterward, the whole nine yards. I was not invited. I don't think this was an exclusionary gesture on Ann's part; she knew I wouldn't be comfortable with such people, and perhaps she knew they wouldn't be comfortable with me. But the Laughlin children had played with the children of the other families, had gone to school with them at fancy boarding schools in Massachusetts, and naturally the parents knew one another. The social fabric of the town, though not confining, was more or less inescapable for the Laughlins. When Jas spoke to me about the local luminaries, he always did so in a self-conscious, ironic way, indicating tacitly that he had to put up with them for Aunt Leila's sake, or for Ann's sake, or for the children's sake, and he would tell me uncomplimentary stories about them, how so-and-so had been found in bed with his wife's chauffeur or such-and-such had jumped her horse into the swimming pool at the country club. But he kept up good relations with them; he passed the time of day with them every morning when he went downtown for his mail and the *Times*; he contributed to local charities, etc. What else could he do?

Well, he could have sold out and moved to California, taking New Directions with him. It would have been an interesting, colorful, and even in some ways practical thing to do. But I'm certain the idea never presented itself seriously to him. Convention, whether social or familial, had a certain importance for Jas. He moved within it as a free agent, yet he required its presence in his life as a defining superficial counterfoil, and probably also as a balancing and supportive control. Why did New Directions not publish the forbidden books of Henry Miller or Nabokov's *Lolita*? These and plenty of other such books were available to him. He read them and admired them. But he was unwilling to risk the legal and judicial consequences that would ensue if he violated the laws governing censorship and public decency, perhaps because he didn't wish to see his family name bruited about in the press in connection with such a scandal – after all, the highly publicized trials ensuing from the publication of Joyce's *Ulysses* in the U.S. were still in recent memory – but actually, I think, he had more subtle and personal reasons. Any kind of public emotional display was repugnant to him, any kind at all. He would have been morti-fied, for example, to find himself on the stand in a courtroom being asked questions about his private sexual proclivities. This didn't keep him from uttering the ordinary indecent innu-endos in ordinary conversation; as long as they were dressed up with style and wit, they were acceptable. But in a courtroom? In any public place? No. Hence the job of publishing *Tropic of Cancer* and *Lolita* went to Barney Rosset of Grove Press, who was willing to endure the legal hassles.

Jas rarely went to church, yet from time to time he professed conventional pieties with apparent ingenuousness, and he kept on good terms with the Congregational minister in Norfolk.

What was Jas thinking at any given time? You could tell if you paid close enough attention to his voice, gesture, expression, his slips of the tongue – or at least you thought you could. But you could never be certain. You concluded, first, that he was a distinctly private person in spite of his public activities and, secondly, that he only committed himself, fully and deliber-ately, in his writing.

Incidentally, Jas was the one who taught me that in the suc-cession of adverbial ordinals it is correct to say "first, secondly, thirdly," etc. I verified this in the big dictionary. Not one in five professional copy editors know it. With Jas anything was ac-ceptable in language, any aberration or vulgarity, provided it was used knowingly and for good effect. Then it was even praiseworthy. But careless or habitual error was an abomina-tion, and the verbal conventions were to be observed strictly. When I did copyediting work for him, I used the Merriam-Webster second international unabridged, and I checked every hyphen, every capitalization.

◇◇◇

The people of Norfolk knew that Jas was a publisher and a famous literary man. When his name appeared in the *Times*, they were pleased, they kidded him about it at the post office. But not one in a hundred of them had ever read a New Directions book, probably not one in five hundred gave a damn this way or that, and Jas acquiesced readily enough. Ideally everyone would read New Directions books, of course. In the real world, however, Jas was a realist, a dedicated one. He was content to submerge himself in the general population. He wanted to be an individual but never a weirdo – definitely not. The story of Immanuel Kant among the Königsburgers was something he relished.

Although Jas and I were friends for fifty years, my own association with New Directions was somewhat like that of the people of Norfolk. I never had an official connection, I was never on the payroll. When I did a job for New Directions, it was a hack job, as I called it, and I was paid a one-time fee. I had been in the office on 14th Street, then later on Eighth Avenue, both before and after my job at Intercultural, and I knew some of the people who worked there – Bob MacGregor, of course, and Peter Glassgold, Griselda Ohannessian, and others. During the past twenty years, when I've given a reading in New York, they've come to it. New Directions published a number of my books.

But I was never a "New Directions author," as I'd have liked to be. I envied my good friend Denise Levertov, who had a stable, reliable relationship with New Directions; Jas would publish practically anything she wrote. I would have given a good deal to have such a relationship with any publisher, instead of scrounging and begging in the literary marketplace. I would show my stuff to Jas from time to time, and sometimes he'd offer to publish it, sometimes he wouldn't. Once he did both: he published half of the manuscript I showed him (*Asphalt*

Georgics) but rejected the other half (*The Oldest Killed Lake in North America*, eventually published by Marilyn Kitchell's Salt-Works Press). His explanation was that my work is only partly experimental, not offbeat enough for an avant-garde publishing house like New Directions. Beyond that, my work didn't sell. Years later, when Jas had retired from many of his functions as a publisher and when I suggested to him that New Directions ought to publish my collected poems, he showed me a note from Griselda saying, in effect, that my work was a drag on the market and New Directions shouldn't take on any such losing proposition.[21] Griselda was right. All she had to do was look at the sales records to see that no book of mine had ever sold more than a few hundred or maybe a thousand copies. But I wish she and Jas had had a little more faith in the importance of what I was doing.[22]

The fact that they didn't was no impediment to my friendship with Jas. For one thing, I knew enough about publishing from my own experience to understand the constraints on any publisher's list of new books. For another, I wasn't sufficiently sure of my own work to disagree with anyone's judgment of it. I knew my poems were off the beaten track, unacceptable to the literary élite in New York, among whom I always felt like a farmer in bib overalls with cowshit on his boots – but I also knew my writing wasn't novel or technically original, and was unacceptable to the Olson-inspired Black Mountain poets and

21. The books have been published by Copper Canyon Press, which has been a great stroke of good fortune for me.

22. Another time, in 1970 or 1971, a book of mine called "Summer '69" was accepted by ND but never published, because a serious upset in the New York office intervened. Somebody absconded with the cash reserves. This was about the time of the economic recession of 1970, which may also have had something to do with it. Such a possibility was hinted at.

the Beats. I received Jas's rejections unquestioningly and with as much equanimity as I could muster. I also was aware that most self-confident poets would consider the rejections good cause for breaking off, for hostility or even public enmity; I'd seen this often enough in my life among the literati. However, for my part I did not want to be a "self-confident poet" – anything but.

One of the things that writers of my generation found most attractive about the avant-garde of literature at midcentury was the sense of solidarity among serious writers. A radical poet like Auden could be published in the same magazine as a conservative poet like Eliot; the intellectual world was equally interested in both. A serious and talented poet always had a place in the community. The fragmentation and factionalism that came in the 1950s and 1960s were a disappointment to us. Jas agreed, or at least I think he did. He supported some of the factionalists, like Ferlinghetti or Duncan, but he personally liked the camaraderie of the 1920s and 1930s. New Directions was devoted, by principle and by name, to new writing, which often meant experimental writing, but at the same time New Directions published Yvor Winters, John Crowe Ransom, Mark Van Doren, Robert Fitzgerald, Richard Eberhart, and many other poets who worked in conventional modes, as well as Pound, Williams, and Rexroth.

But what I want to get at here is not the philosophy of publishing at New Directions, but my peculiar friendship with James Laughlin. I was at a remove from New Directions, usually quite a distant remove. Sometimes Jas would talk about problems that arose at the office, and he liked to have someone at his side who was not attached to the office but who could commiserate with him intelligently about the burdens and inanities of the office, but usually he dismissed these problems, even the most interesting, as workaday routine, boring and not worth discussing. He would rather talk about some favorite author of the past, like Saint-Simon, whose *Mémoires* he quoted often, especially the salacious bits or the buffooneries of court etiquette at Versailles, than about Nabokov or John Hawkes or the incompetence of the bookkeeper.

I saw the publisher at work, of course, his desk heaped with manuscripts, his briefcase bulging with royalty accounts. When he talked with me about New Directions, however, it was usually a question of something new he wanted to do, like *A New Directions Reader* or a program to publish translations of new European fiction.

In the early days Jas kept the royalty accounts himself, and sent out royalty statements and checks from the post office in Norfolk. The checks were written in his own hand against his account at the bank in Canaan or Winsted. Later he let others do the accounting, but he continued to write the checks himself, toward the end in a minuscule shaky hand. Most of these checks were scarcely worth the writing, or the receiving. My checks were usually for $22.10 or something like that. Most other poets got no more than I did. But part of Jas's devotion to New Directions was in his meticulous personal attention to the smallest details and his belief that even the most obviously philanthropic program of passionate publishing should be administered in a strictly businesslike way. Most of the time New Directions lost money; the focus of managerial energy was on keeping the loss to a minimum. Sometimes New Directions made money, when authors like Dylan Thomas and Tennessee Williams were discovered, unexpectedly, to be popular. How it all balanced out in the end is unknown to me, but clearly – and no doubt whatever exists about this – New Directions was not intended to be a profit-making enterprise. Breaking even, without any return to the publisher, would be a triumph, and my guess is that this was accomplished. In any case the firm is still continuing, because in his will Jas established a trust to oversee the operation of the company for a while still to come.

As for the books themselves, my own experience with them is typical, I imagine. At school, including my undergraduate years, and in the army I learned nothing about contemporary poetry. As a young man twenty-five years old in 1946 I had heard of only two living poets, Carl Sandburg and Robert Frost, both of whom I thought were oddballs in one sense or another. I thought poetry was dead. I thought it had died with the poets my father admired, the Rossettis, Dowson, Swinburne, the author of *The Rose-Jar*, which was a book of abominable sonnets published by Mosher of Portland; I found it on the family bookshelf. I simply did not know that a good many people were writing serious poetry in this country. The only contemporary poems I saw were those in my mother's magazines, *Good Housekeeping* and *Ladies' Home Journal.* Then when I went to Chicago, in 1946 after I was discharged from the army, I found a copy of the beautiful 1938 edition of Williams's *Collected Poems*, designed by Peter Beilenson and printed at the Walpole Press, in a bookstore on the south side, and my education began. From that time on I read the poets published by New Directions almost religiously, not only the giants of the past but young poets like Patchen and Elliott Coleman and many, many others.

◇◇◇

Gertrude is out of the hospital, at home in Meadow House.[23] Being tended by a full-time nurse whose name is Eva. Eva

23. March 19, 1998.

speaks with an accent that sounds Austrian or Swiss. Gertrude speaks in a voice that is barely audible, a whisper. She says she cannot remember anything during the whole week in hospital, which must mean she was unconscious most of the time, very ill. But I'm still not clear about details. From the beginning Gertrude's illness has been obscured in mystery; either she has been bamboozling me, or others have been bamboozling her – or, I suppose, both. She has suffered terribly, however, no doubt of that. First, the failure of vision, then the lung problems – pneumonia, asthma, cancer. She used to say, last summer and fall, that she was the one in Meadow House who was ill, and at least some of the sympathy going to Jas should be given to her. She said this in her usual ironic, good-humored way, pouting demonstratively like a little girl; but she said it. In some part she meant it. And she was right.

There she is, the lifelong mistress of a great man and eventually his wife, now an emaciated miserable woman, ill and alone (except for the hired nurse) in a big house in a forgotten and forgettable corner of the land. Nor do I mean to say she was only an adjunct. On the contrary she was an artist, a designer, one of the best, indispensably engaged in the great endeavor of publishing good books in America.

And here am I, an old man with shaky hands and failing breath writing at the end of the century, the end of the millennium. It is impossible not to feel the gloom. Our great endeavor has come to an end, not with a whimper, not with a bang either, but in a huge diffusion. Literally hundreds and hundreds of little presses are publishing poetry every day, where once we could count such presses on the fingers of our hands. The poetry itself is precious, irrelevant, pedantic, and dull. It pours into my little house in upstate New York as if through all the doors and windows, just as it pours like streams of flotsam down every gutter and sewer in the country. My friend Don Hall, in his dearly insufferable optimism, would say it's all for the best; I'm sure he has statistics to "prove" that the poetic impulse is alive and well in the U.S.A. Maybe it is. Maybe the "poetic impulse" is a constant in human psychology, always at the same level; I wouldn't be surprised. Always churning away. Does it make a difference that these thousands and thousands of poets are working now with a very imperfect understanding of craft and no real knowledge of the tradition? As one who knew Shapiro, Lowell, Schwartz, Roethke, Rukeyser, Levertov, Bishop, Tate, Jarrell, Bogan – well, as one who had a glimpse of the great endeavor in the sum of its artistic and intellectual entirety, before the great academic takeover, I must say it makes a difference to me. A big difference. Cataclysm. *Kataklusmos*. The Flood.

Rap music is not the blues.

Gertrude said she is scared. I told her I'm scared too. I told her I love her. I told her I will come to see her as soon as she is able to receive anyone. She answered feebly, but for a moment she seemed glad to hear from me. A couple of distraught survivors.

◇◇◇

One time, after I had moved to Vermont, Ann and Jas were on the road in her gray Falcon, she driving, Jas in the passenger seat doing his royalty statements. They stopped to see me. Rose Marie made tea, but essentially Ann and Jas wanted no refreshment. Jas came out to the cowshed – so called because it had been a one-cow barn in the frugal times of family self-sufficiency seventy or eighty years ago – only seventy or eighty? – yes, so quickly the times have changed – Jas, then, came out to see me in the cowshed, a towering figure in that cramped space. He sat, gangly, in my old oak rocker. He looked around at the makeshift bookshelves, the rusty filing cabinet, the cracked cast-iron stove, the strings hanging from the ceiling with papers clipped to them, the wires running everywhere, the woodbox, the ash bucket, the old typewriter, the lamp with the lampshade made by Rose Marie from pages of an art catalog. "So this is where you do it," he said. He seemed impressed.

Though he threatened to come and visit me several other times, this was the only time he actually did it.

It was winter. I recall the gray Falcon disappearing slowly down the old gravel road through a curtain of falling snow.

◇◇◇

Jas wasn't writing much during the time I lived in Norfolk. He didn't say anything about this, but I suspect he suffered from a lifelong depression about his writing, perhaps stemming from that cruel remark of Pound's when Jas was a college boy, but probably rooted more deeply than that. When Jas first visited Rapallo and showed Ez (as we called him) his manuscripts, the great man had told him to quit writing and go home; he had told him to concentrate his energy and wealth on publishing the modern masters. It was indeed a cruel thing to say, as a good number of people since then have pointed out, yet quite in keeping with Pound's temperament, his autocraticism, his impresarial and manipulative desire to help himself and his friends. Besides, Ez was crazy; Jas told me he could see the clear signs of it during his first visits to Rapallo in the middle 1930s. Pound would lie in his hammock and say nothing hour after hour. Paranoid schizophrenia, that's what it was called, though today the clinical terminology has doubtless changed. At any rate it's very plain that Jas was extraordinarily reticent about his own writing during most of his life, until in old age he became more confident and, in a way, more ambitious.

The question, however, is more complicated than that. He was the founder and head of the chief avant-garde publishing house in the Anglo-American world. If he published his own poetry, he would be accused of literary egomania. If he let other people publish it, he would be accused of intraliterary back-patting and nepotism. In either case, he would be accused of using his wealth and position to serve himself. Jas was extremely – and I do mean extremely – sensitive to any such imputation. Jas was a little crazy himself – who isn't? – repressed and inhibited and melancholy from his earliest days on earth, and Pound's opprobrium merely activated an enormous personal mechanism of insecurity.

When did Jas begin writing? He never said. I suspect it was not in childhood, though it might have been if his mother or Aunt Leila encouraged him, but rather when he was in secondary school at that place in Switzerland or at Choate under the tutelage of Dudley Fitts. By the time he was an undergraduate at Harvard he was writing poetry seriously, committedly. Fitts had introduced him to Pound, Williams, Cummings and other modern poets, and Jas was smitten. He worked out his own prosodic formula at an early age, and as far as I know it was absolutely unique with him. He called it "typewriter prosody." Once he showed me the Xerox of an article about it, I think from the Harvard *Crimson.* The idea was simple enough: he wrote his poems on a typewriter, with which he was adept, and the first line of each poem, as it occurred to him randomly, established the length of every other line in the rest of the poem, which could deviate from the first line by no more than two typewritten characters in either direction. Hyphens were permissible at line endings. It was a rigid enough metrical scheme; one has to go to Asian calligraphic poems or cuneiform texts to find other prosodies based on mere appearance. Yet the poetry of the moderns, especially Williams, was a big influence on Jas, and clearly the alignments in some of that poetry were established typographically, not metrically in the conventional sense; that is to say, Williams made runover lines to suit his eye as well as his ear. Beyond this, syllabic verse, as in the poems of Marianne Moore, was in the air, so to speak, and the idea of counting characters was not far removed from the idea of counting syllables.

Wherever it came from, typewriter prosody was a good deal more than undergraduate bravado, as it may appear to be at first. Jas used it all his life. I believe – indeed, I have argued the point in print – that he used it *poetically*, not just mechanically.

What does this mean? I remember one time when Denise Levertov had been reading some of my poems in manuscript, she remarked on how the rhyme and meter I was using had "forced" me to make felicitous phrasings. I preferred, of course, to think that my verbal imagination had produced these felicities in tandem with the prosodic requirements, as in the case, e.g., of William Shakespeare. Jas thought of his typewriter prosody in the same terms. If the requirements of his artificially established line produced effects of syntax and enjambment that were poetically effective, this was indeed poetry – the consequence of sensibility and imagination. This is what the hard craft of poetry consists of, as Pound himself had maintained and asserted, the eloquent distribution of language within a metrical preconception. Jas wanted, desired, needed the artifice as a challenge to his poetic ear, and he believed Dante had done the same thing with *terza rima*.

I couldn't have agreed more. Everything I knew about poetry, from reading as well as from my own practice, confirmed this. Pound had said that no such thing as free verse can exist, properly speaking, even though he himself was a major practitioner of what most people called by that name. "Heave out the pentameter," he had said, not "Heave out the artifice." The confusion over this in American literature of the twentieth century was, and is, staggering. Yet it's a simple distinction.

What I found in Jas's poems, in spite of the artificial prosody, in spite of the plain diction and syntax on which he insisted – he called it "natural" – was a lyrical voice deriving straight from the late medieval and Renaissance European tradition. And if I had known more about Greek and Latin poetry, I expect I'd have found an important influence there as well. At the same time, however, the "voice" was very much his own.

Jas published his early poems reticently. Nevertheless, he did publish them – or some of them. Several small books appeared, usually in conjunction with a European publisher such as Giovanni Scheiwiller of Milan, or the Stamperia Valdonega of Verona, or the Gaberbocchus Press of London. The books appeared in the United States under the imprint of New Directions, but they were never advertised, they were published in small print runs, and in effect they were gift editions for Jas to give to his friends. The first book of any importance was *Some Natural Things* (1945), which was followed by a *Selected Poems*, only forty pages, in 1959. I read these poems with care and admiration. "The Mountain Afterglow," which was the opening poem in the *Selected*, seemed to me as expressive a poem on a perennial theme as any I had ever read. When I came to edit my anthology years later, *The Voice That Is Great Within Us*, I included it.

Somehow the poetry of Williams, Olson, Ginsberg, O'Hara and others, though through absolutely no fault of theirs, has led young people to believe that a good poem is an artless poem.

We see the massive result today in hundreds and hundreds of publications, in which carelessness seems actually to be prized. To me and to other poets of my generation this is strange. When we were young, we thought the opposite: that the art of poetry was in concealing the art, which was harder to do than revealing it could ever be. As Yeats said – and we never forgot – you must get down on your hands and knees and work like a washerwoman to make your poem appear as if it came without effort.

Jas did not show me any manuscripts, aside from blurbs, intros, etc., while I was in Norfolk. I knew he had manuscripts – cached in that vault in the back room. He told me about some of the prose things he had written but didn't wish to publish, at least not yet, especially pieces about Williams. I liked his prose, had admired it from my first reading of his introductions to the New Directions annuals in the 1940s, and I was eager to read what he had written about Williams, Pound, and others. But he never let me. Not until much later. As for his poems, if he was writing any during that period he kept them to himself.

Not long after I moved to Vermont, however, he began to send me manuscripts of new poems and ask me what I thought about them. It was natural for me to make suggestions, at first tentatively and hesitantly, but as he accepted more and more of what I recommended, and as he became more and more trusting and appreciative, I became more confident. Often when I received a new poem from him, I would twirl a sheet of paper into my typewriter out in the cowshed, type out the first line, and then proceed to re-align, re-phrase, re-work the whole poem, sticking to his prosody. I liked doing this. In fact, I wrote a number of poems of my own in blatant imitation of Jas's method. And I liked his voice too, though it wasn't even close to my own natural voice. I found I could mimic him. In truth, I was a natural mimic – in writing, not in speech – and many of my own poems were done in other people's voices, so that when I revised his poems – or anyone else's – I was doing the same thing I did in composing my own, writing as someone else might write. I could produce a "Laughlin poem" any time I wanted to. Jas himself would be astonished and delighted, and would tell me so in his responding notes and letters. This continued for many years, until in the 1980s and 1990s I was spending a great deal of time on his poems, and when they were big poems, like the sections of his "Byways," this was a definite assignment and I was paid for doing it. The pay was small, as usual with Jas, but it was sent meticulously, and sometimes when he was particularly pleased – because in addition to revising I often prepared final, camera-ready copy for him on my computer – he'd send me an extra check.

Jas called me a "poetry doctor." He told me that in the old days Marianne Moore had been his best doctor, which I can easily believe. As I've said, her syllabic prosody was not far from his typewriter prosody. In addition, she had the right temperament for such work, and she was a first-rate editor. Jas befriended her, though he never published her; he didn't need to, she was well-published already by others. From time to time Jas and Ann would take Miss Moore, as she was called then, to baseball games at Ebbets Field so she could root for her beloved Dodgers. Their relationship was close and affectionate.

Jas himself was a Pittsburgh fan. Over and over he lamented the bad luck and bad judgment of the Pirates.

◇◇◇

Wonza's brother was killed in Florida. Shot by a white man for no reason at a rural filling station somewhere in the barbaric part of the state. The shooter was not the owner of the filling station, and Wonza's brother had merely stopped to buy gas for his car. Probably the guy was drunk, venting his redneck rage in an act of random brutality.

This was in the early 1960s when the modern phase of the civil rights movement was just gearing up. As someone who had been attached to an earlier phase of the movement, Eleanor Roosevelt's Southern Regional Council before the war, I knew that such atrocities occurred far more often in the South than most Northerners could contemplate in their still essentially Lockean view of human goodness. I remembered the time when I was a student at Chapel Hill, circa 1937, and a group of Southern boys had got into a stake truck with their shotguns, then driven down the main street of Carrboro, which was an almost entirely black community at that time, and had shot everything that moved. Fun and games, it was called, or keeping the boogers in their place.

Wonza was shocked, grief stricken, and of course very angry. All of us were appalled and shaken. Wonza went down to Florida to spend some time with the rest of her family, and Jas and Ann made arrangements with a high-powered firm of attorneys to pursue the case and obtain a little justice or at least a little revenge. But it dragged on interminably. Wonza came back to Norfolk and resumed her life there. Eventually a trial was held and the shooter was duly acquitted by a jury of his peers. It was a predictable outcome.

It was also, of course, the sort of event that remains forever unresolved and deeply troubling in one's consciousness.

Wonza and Arthur, her husband, lived by the highway on the west end of Norfolk, as I've said already, beside the river where the land slopes down steeply into the valley. Their house was a two-story house faced in dark gray stucco with a porch in front and the river behind. A mill was nearby, a three-story building with small windows lined up blankly on its facade, one of the thousands and thousands of mills that had propelled the economic life of New England in the old days – every river had its contingent, and almost every brook – small factories taking their energy from the power of running water – what a sensible idea! But by 1960 most of them were out of business. I don't remember what Arthur did, except that he wasn't employed by the Laughlins. I didn't see him often. A few years later he was diagnosed with cancer from a mole on his arm that had turned skeptical, as we used to say, and in no time, it seemed, he was dead. The house by the river became too much for Wonza. A small house was built for her beside Mountain Road on the way to the village, near where Theodore lived.[24] It was a modest one-story brick house, but attractive and comfortable, with a yard and garden. Wonza was proud of it. She liked to have visitors and she always welcomed us warmly when we turned up in Norfolk. As she became older she reduced her working hours at Meadow House and then retired altogether. But she and Arthur had had no children, and I think, I fear, she was very lonely at the end.

Ann was the one who conceived the idea for Wonza's house and supervised its construction – and paid for it too from her own money. I bet she had a hell of a fine time doing it. If the notion hadn't been so anti-Radcliffean, Ann would have made a splendid architect or engineer – or at least a contractor. She had exactly the right temperament for it.

Wonza was famous for her pastry. Whenever she made blintzes for the people at Meadow House, she would make a few extra, three or four, and send them in a basket to the cottage

24. Theodore Silvernayle was one of the native Norfolkians who had worked at Robin Hill and continued working on the estate after Aunt Leila's death.

by Theodore for Rose Marie and me. They were delicious, and we were genuinely grateful.

I used to sit in the kitchen at Meadow House and talk with Wonza. She was intelligent, literate, a woman of vigorous attitudes and opinions. She would give me coffee and cookies. Wonza was always aware of her status as a "servant," aware of a certain line she could not cross, much more aware of it than I was; yet we became good friends. I mean we were personally engaged in one another's lives. Is this what was meant in the Old South by the "mutual regard" of the races? I suppose so. Other black women from Florida worked at Meadow House too. The oldest was Annie Dixon, I think, who was arthritic and had a lot of pain in her hands; she went to Boston once for special treatment, but it didn't help her. She laughed at the doctors and called them knuckleheads. Then she retired back to Florida. Another was Mahalia, a very majestic woman with snow-white hair. After a while Mahalia left Meadow House and went to work for another family on the north side of town, among the Dolittlers. When I visited her there, as I did whenever I was in Norfolk, she would complain about boredom. She'd take me out to the back of the estate where she worked and show me the pond, which was well populated with frogs. She had a rod about four feet long with a rope tied to it and a stone tied to the end of the rope. She would stalk around the edge of the pond and when she saw a frog she'd swing the rod and try to hit it with the stone. "Chunking the frogs," she called it. If she ever hit one, which I doubt, it probably wouldn't have hurt much. A silly pastime, as she said, but it made her laugh and eased the boredom a little.

Through Wonza, Annie, and Mahalia I learned a little about the life of the underclass in Norfolk. Not that I was ever assimilated to it, any more than I was assimilated to the life of the upperclass. I was an outsider, regarded by all, or almost all, as neutral and amiable. Mostly the servants of Norfolk were blacks, and of course they came from somewhere else. They were a community in exile. They made up a society of their own as well as they could, an invisible network beneath the super-structure of white affluence, held together by friendships, mu-tual memories, language, and, of course, their church. Some of the women were married, like Wonza, but most were not, like Mahalia. These people were comfortable and reasonably well off, at least compared to most other African-Americans; yet ex-cept in the kitchens and pantries of the town they were indeed invisible, one never saw them in any public gathering – even their church was somewhere else, in Canaan or Winsted. It was the kind of social condition, at both ends of the spectrum, that might have been exploited for a television sitcom, in the manner of the BBC, if anyone had taken the trouble to do it. And ex-ploitation would have been at the heart of it too: no matter how complex and intricate the relationships, it was still exploitation. I had read my Marx when I was fifteen, and I knew. But did I do anything about it? Except in my way of personal amiability and openness, no.

Did Jas do anything? At a time of crisis, such as the death of Wonza's brother, he did what he practically could. And at other times he smiled and said good morning to the black women in his house. I never saw him make any real gesture of personal concern toward them, however, nor did I see such gestures to-ward Theodore or any of the other people on the staff. He would have said that personal engagement with the workers was impractical and unfeasible. He would have said the same thing about personal engagement with nearly anyone.

Jas regarded the larger scene with a kind of amused con-tempt. The barbarisms of the redneck element in federal politics,

from Tom Dewey and Joe McCarthy to Jesse Helms and Newt
Gingrich, were an abomination to him, as they were to all of us.
He believed in the humanity and practicality of Social Credit,
though his belief became less resolute as he grew older, and not
only because of Pound's influence; he had read the works of
Major Douglas and other theorists, and he followed the affairs
of the *Créditistes* in Canada with interest. He thought the social-
ization of banking was probably a good idea, in other words,
and on that template he accepted the feasibility of social-
ization in other sectors of public and social service: communi-
cations, medicine, education, etc. But when it came to the
"means of production"? I'm not sure. I suspect he was a mod-
erate Manchester liberal, and would have defended the rights
of private property and private enterprise. But mainly he was,
as I say, amused and contemptuous when it came to political
affairs. I doubt that he voted in national elections, though he
probably did in local ones. Like all of us – conservatives, social-
ists, Trotskyites, anarchists – he knew that good order was
more a question of cultural than of political attachments, and
that the pursuit of happiness depended more on esthetic and
spiritual than on material values. And as the second half of the
twentieth century unfolded, he became more and more disillu-
sioned, more and more hopeless. He still bought the *Times*
every morning and watched the TV news every evening; he
liked to smoke a cigar and make caustic comments while the
news unrolled. He was not uninterested. But as a poet he
would have said, in essence, that the real tragedy of human ex-
istence is the boy on the nightly news who falls down a well in
Texas, not the inanities of Congress. He would have said that
the plight of the rich man and the poor man is the same, and is,
in a world of violence and brutality, irreparable.

◇◇◇

Jas at work. In the living room at Meadow House. He'd sit be-
hind his desk, a good-sized piece of furniture, where he could
look out to the meadow easily. Off to one side the television
would be turned on: baseball, football, tennis, whatever. He'd
be smoking a cigar. He might be dictating letters – the audio of
the TV was turned down low enough so that the Dictaphone
wouldn't pick it up – or messing around with papers. Some-
times I'd be working with him, seated in the armchair by the
coffee table. Jas would have asked me to read a particular
manuscript or help him in concocting a ticklish letter or jacket
blurb – something like that.

When Jas had finished with a cigar, he'd rear back and
throw the stub at the fireplace across the room. He had a good
arm; usually the stub landed in the fireplace. Sometimes it
would bounce off onto the floor, and when I'd begin to pick it
up Jas would say: "Let it be. The maid'll get it in the morning."
Jas liked to smoke his cigar right down to the bitter end. He'd
keep lighting it, even when the match-flame came up against
his nose. If he'd had a beard, he would have immolated himself.
Once he came close – sometime in the late 1980s. He was read-
ing and smoking in the living room, and Ann was elsewhere in
the house; in fact she was in bed in the downstairs guest room
with her cancer, occupied with a long phone conversation. Jas
dropped his burning cigar into his armchair and didn't notice it.
The chair and the papers around it began to smolder. Jas and
one of the maids tried to move the burning chair outdoors, but
it wouldn't fit through the doorway. Then Jas went for a fire
extinguisher, but all the extinguishers were at the caretaker's
cottage for recharging; they'd been there for months. This is
what I was told by a third person who was in a position to know

the truth, at any rate. Jas himself confided to me that he had accidentally dropped a lighted match in his wastebasket, and he told me to keep mum about it. Because of the insurance? Damage to the living room was severe, and to parts of the rest of the house as well, burning up some of the wonderful paintings, destroying most of the collection of classical texts on the living-room shelves. It's a wonder the whole house didn't burn. It's a wonder Jas and Ann and the maids weren't smothered in their beds, their bodies charred and blistered. Well, by good fortune they all escaped. Ann was even able to rescue a couple of Klees that were hanging on the wall of the guest room. I don't know if the insurance paid off or not, but first-rate workers were hired to restore the house, which they did quickly and perfectly, as least as far as I could tell. But of course some of the most important losses were unrestorable. You wouldn't have known it, however, if you had visited Meadow House a year later. The place looked exactly the same, other books were found to fill the bookshelves, a new Marin was bought to replace the one that burned on the living-room wall, even the former furniture in the living room was duplicated exactly. Jas and the rest of the occupants carried on their lives as if nothing had happened. Perhaps this is the main point of the whole episode.

When Jas smoked his pipe – he alternated pipes and cigars about half-and-half – he would relight the pipe a dozen times for every bowl of tobacco consumed. He did it with a quick, impatient movement, shaking the match to put out the flame, squinting his eyes against the smoke. Sometimes he did drop lighted matches into wastebaskets.

Tobacco was Jas's only "substance abuse," unless you count sex. He was moderate with alcohol. A glass of wine at dinner, perhaps a shot of Courvoisier at night to help him sleep. He liked to drink milk, and often had a glass of milk and a cookie for a snack. He had other tastes that seemed peculiar to me. He was fond of junket, for instance. I don't know if that's a trade name or not, but it refers to a somewhat sweetish, pastel-colored pudding made with lots of milk that used to be fed to children in the old days. My mother fed it to me. But Jas was the only adult I've ever run into who kept on eating it. To me, the taste was altogether bland and uninteresting.

Around 1970 Jas's depression became worse. I take it that a deep underlying despondency that had always been buried in his psyche broke to the surface. He complained of fatigue and inability to work. His shrink put him on lithium, a powerful drug used mostly to control the mania of manic-depressive psychosis. I don't know why, but it worked well for Jas and he was enthusiastic about it. He recommended it to me and offered to pay the expense of getting started, the clinical testing and blood-monitoring that are necessary for a while at the beginning. I never did it. I've always gotten along on ordinary antidepressants, Nardil, Elavil, Pamelor, Wellbutrin, Prozac, etc.[25] For fifteen years or so the lithium worked beautifully for Jas, he was well pleased with it. Then, inevitably, it wore out. The effect diminished and side effects became more pronounced, especially a tremor that made it almost impossible for him to write legibly by hand. The doctors began testing and experimenting, and he went along with them, somewhat reluctantly. Toward the end of his life he had an array of pill bottles on the kitchen windowsill that suggested a pharmacopoeia, and every morning, with his soft-boiled egg and juice, he'd swallow pill after pill. The depression was never as well controlled again after he was taken off lithium, and the shakes continued until his death.

25. For some years I've taken 30 mg. of Prozac a day, and it works well enough.

The truth is, I presume, that Jas was a manic-depressive, or as we say now a bipolar, schizophrenic and delusionary to one degree or another. But such things are unmeasurable. He relied on his shrink in later years, but he was never hospitalized for his depression, or even close to it. His illness, in the clinical sense, was never recognized by his friends.

When we were working in the living room, at some point Jas would look up from his desk and make a huffing noise in his throat. "Screw it, Hayden," he'd say. "Let's go swimming." Or skiing, as the case may have been.

◇◇◇

In ordinary conversation Jas used as much casual and gratuitous sexual innuendo as everyone else did in those days. I don't get out much, but I presume everyone still does. In spite of recent reforms in our thinking about such matters, it's part of human mentality.

One time at Intercultural, Gertrude and Jas were in my office to discuss the graphics that would accompany an essay on painting, reproductions of the artist's work. To meet a particular need, Jas suggested that we use a tipped-in, folded, three-panel insert, in full color on coated stock. "You could pull it out – forgive the expression – like an accordion," he said. Gertrude chuckled and I smiled and Jas remained absolutely deadpan.

I remember this not because it has any special significance but because it seems generally characteristic.

◇◇◇

Norfolk was a fine place to spend a couple of years. I couldn't have been luckier. Every season was a pleasure. The entire sloping ground between Robin Hill and the cottage had been planted with azaleas, for instance, and in spring they bloomed spectacularly in many colors. The view from the back of the cottage faced west, so that often in the evening we saw sunsets, equally spectacular, vaulting above the flowers. The rhododendron in our front yard was more muted but still very abundant, very colorful. The woods were full of mountain laurel that flowered beautifully in June. During the summer we had a munificence of interesting wildflowers – Turk's-cap lilies, cardinal flowers, orchises of several kinds, wild sunflowers by the roadside, fireweed, joe-pye weed, butterfly weed and steeplebush in the fields, etc. – and in the fall I knew just where to find a patch of fringed gentian – the loveliest wildflower of the east – on the road to Falls Village. And we had an abundance of songbirds too. We were far enough south to be visited in summer by some of my favorite species, like Carolina wrens, towhees, and little green herons, which I never saw after we moved to Vermont.[26] And we had all the usual northeastern summer birds, very colorful, goldfinches, indigo buntings, tanagers, redstarts, orioles, etc. The woods were full of animals. I saw foxes, porcupines, beaver on Tobey Pond, plenty of rabbits and woodchucks and white-tailed deer. At night you could hear the bucks snorting in the dark around the cottage, and if you shone your flashlight among the trees, you would pick up many reflecting eyes.

The cottage had a small but pleasant yard in back, against the wall of the stable and carriage house. We planted dahlias in an old flower bed there and they did well. Jas came and looked at them, and said that's the way a flower bed should be, which was gratifying. We had weeded it well. He would fold himself

26. But in compensation I saw many arctic species during the winter in Vermont: snowy owls, pine grosbeaks, snow buntings, longspurs, crossbills, redpolls, and others.

into a lawn chair like some great industrial machine coming to rest at the end of the workday, take out a cigar and light it, polish his glasses on the end of his tie, and sip the lemonade Rose Marie had provided. He seemed altogether at ease, which was uncommon, and we took pleasure from it. He would talk at length about anything at all.

I suppose often in the presence of great men one forgets their greatness. Part of the greatness, after all, is their unassuming, easy manner. What Jas had done in his life already, in 1960 when he was still in his forties, was phenomenal. If Ezra Pound was the inventor of modern poetry, as I once wrote, Jas was its great advocate and disseminator, the statesman of modern literature in America. Remember that in the 1920s E.E. Cummings had submitted one of his books to every publishing house in New York without an acceptance. It was rejected by them all. T.S. Eliot, that staid, gentlemanly eminence, was still regarded as a radical, untrustworthy if not downright disgusting. The "Bohemian" – Edna St. Vincent Millay, for instance, or Vachel Lindsay – was anathema in American universities. Jas changed all that, almost single-handedly. I don't mean to slight in the least the extraordinary things done by the poets themselves or the critics[27] – this should go without saying – but Jas was the engineer and architect of the new enlightenment. Yet when we were sitting there among the flowers in back of the cottage, we were just a couple of guys talking about politics or baseball or maybe a new book.

On the other hand I never became totally unaware of the sense of power exuded in the presence of Jas. This was a man

27. Allen Tate once said to me that the task of his generation had been to change public taste in America from that of Cambridge in 1870 to that of intelligent readers everywhere in 1945, especially as evidenced in schools and universities. By 1960 the change had begun.

who could do things that no one else could do. It was a question not simply of wealth but of intellect and energy. Of status: his place in the world was exalted. My place was like a grain of sand on the shore. This was so obvious that it became almost forgotten, almost taken for granted – almost, but not quite.

Jas knew not only Pound and Eliot, Cocteau and Gide, Stein and Hemingway. He dined with Charles de Gaulle – or if he didn't it was because he didn't want to. He could knock on any door in the literate Western world, and a good many in the East as well, and receive a welcome. Yet when we were sitting there in Norfolk, that little corner of nowhere, the great apparatus of Western culture seemed remote.

At the same time one must acknowledge that what Jas accomplished had little to do, essentially and ultimately, with status or power. It had to do with hard work. It had to do with a degree of effort which I think young people today – my graduate students when I was teaching at Syracuse, for instance – cannot begin to imagine. A stupendous effort. Not that the young people are to blame for their innocence; they are products of their time – lazy and greedy, concerned to discover the easiest way to upgrade their "careers." Certainly this is one of the notable ways in which life in the United States has changed.

As for myself personally, I made a little progress during my sojourn in Norfolk. After two years I still could not walk more than thirty yards in a public place; the distance from the drugstore to the post office defeated me, I was completely dependent on the automobile, but at least I could walk by myself in the woods and fields, I could sit at the dinner table in Meadow House without unbearable tension. I was ready, in other words, to make a further foray. I didn't know this, I didn't think of my life in those terms. I lived from day to day. But Jas knew it – or at least I believe this was how he was thinking.

93

One day in late winter Jas took me aside and told me that he had hired a new person to be gardener and groundskeeper and general handyman. This new person was married and needed the cottage to live in. There was no urging, no coercion of any kind whatsoever. Nevertheless, the implication was clear. In April, Rose Marie, the Bo, and I went touring in northern Vermont and found our new home, and in late May we moved.

◇◇◇

In the old days at Intercultural the women used to say they were pleased when Jas came home from one of his overseas excursions because they enjoyed the aroma of his cigar in the hallway.

We were, in fact, a compatible and contented crew at Intercultural. In addition to the Englishwoman who was secretary to Jas, our staff comprised three others: Jacqui Matisse,[28] Mary Coxe, and Hannah Kaufman. Jacqui was a good-looking, gracious Frenchwoman who had modeled as a child for her famous grandfather. Her father was the proprietor of an important gallery on 57th Street. Mary Coxe was a young blonde, Waspy in appearance but not in manner. She was married to a graduate student at Union Theological Seminary, and she spent her spare moments in the office making colorful ecclesiastical stoles for him. When he graduated they went off to Alaska to serve a mission among the unhappy Inuits, and they gave me their cat, a handsome long-haired gray tabby named Oliver. I changed his name to Tolliver, and he was with me for many years afterward. Hannah Kaufman was my secretary. I had hired her from among a number of candidates sent by an agency because I recognized in her a kindred spirit: during the

28. How I came to forget Jacqui in the opening part of this narrative defeats me.

interview she was almost tongue-tied with anxiety. I was right about this, and we became good friends.

Other people were in and out of the office regularly. Delmore Schwartz came a couple of afternoons a week to write one-paragraph book reviews, which were published in *Perspectives*. Delmore was a certifiable nut, of course, and when he flipped out he did outrageous things. He was famous for the time when he stood in the middle of a Manhattan street and loudly denounced Nelson Rockefeller for stealing his wife. Less publicly, he made the same accusation against others, including Jas. But Jas continued to support him, directly and indirectly, as with the little job at Intercultural, for which Delmore was paid, not bountifully but well enough. Almost anyone else could have done the work more expeditiously and just as competently. Delmore was on his good behavior in the office, of course, because he came in the afternoons before he had begun drinking seriously. But sometimes after work he and I would go to a bar on Madison that I favored and have a drink or two and talk about poetry and baseball. He was a bumbling, good-humored guy, full of suppressed vanity and resentment; but when he was sober he suppressed it well.

The designer Alvin Lustig came to the office sometimes, and sometimes I went to his. He was very helpful with matters of design and production. He was a dapper little guy, spotless and almost clinical in his appearance. He wrote with a gold pen and he wore gold cuff links in his starched cuffs. In his office, which was somewhere in the maze of streets around Madison and Lexington in the 50s, his worktable was an enormous slab of white polished marble. He spoke with a slight German or Austrian accent. He had been greatly important to New Directions in the preceding years, creating a style of bookcover that was unusual, attractive, and easily identifiable.

Ping Ferry came to the office once to speak with me, I don't remember why. Afterward he reported to Jas that I was a "cold fish." No doubt I was.

Some people thought that Intercultural was in the business of giving grants and fellowships, though we weren't. We had applicants and sycophants coming into the office frequently. One was Tambimuttu, the Indian poet who had established *Poetry London* after the war, an important magazine, and then had moved it to New York. He came with his wife in tow, a very beautiful little woman with the traditional spot of rouge on her forehead; she always walked behind Tambi and she said absolutely nothing, she was as silent as the wallpaper. But Tambi would stay for hours sometimes, talking and talking, ingratiating himself.

Once a strikingly handsome woman came, demanding to speak with me. She was dressed beautifully in gray and black, and she had a black eye patch over one eye. She had black hair, black eyes, and a smooth ivory complexion. She exuded sexual power more compellingly than any other woman I've ever met, bar none. She wanted money for a dance group. I told her we didn't do that kind of thing. After she left, Mary, Hannah, and Jacqui let out a collective "Whew," and looked at me as if they were surprised to find me still alive.

From the standpoint of work, the worst day at Intercultural was St. Patrick's Day, when for hours the parade went banging and braying past on Fifth Avenue, just under our windows. We watched for a while. Then we shut up shop and went home.

At that time I was writing book reviews for *The Nation* and was friendly with Margaret Marshall, the literary editor. Margaret lived in a charming walk-up apartment on St. Mark's Place, where she held parties from time to time, wonderful parties. That's where I met Auden and Saul Bellow. Irving Howe was there. Also Baziotes, the painter, who came from Pittsburgh and looked like a steelworker, with squared-off shoulders and strong, stubby hands; he liked to lindy, and he'd put a Basie record on Margaret's phonograph and go jitterbugging all over her apartment, with or without a partner – cutting a rug, as we used to say. Margaret's rugs were pretty well cut. I liked Baziotes' paintings a good deal, and I liked knowing a painter who could make a living from his work. I liked Margaret too, and apparently she liked me, even though I was half-loaded and sat in a dark corner most of the time. But I wasn't totally antisocial. Later, when Margaret was fired from her job, I joined others in protesting to the brass at *The Nation*. Clearly her section of the magazine, the back-of-the-book, as we called it, was more interesting – better written and better edited – than the front.

I can't remember if Paul Goodman came to those parties, but I saw him fairly often elsewhere. Sometimes we'd have a drink together at the outdoor café in front of the hotel on lower Fifth, just off Washington Square. Sometimes I went to his apartment on 11th Avenue near 23rd Street. Paul's son Mathew, whose death years later evoked one of Paul's most memorable poems, was then a little boy, maybe two or three years old.

Eleanore Ray was another who appeared in the office frequently. She was from New Jersey and worked in a midtown magazine office. Somewhat awkwardly, I was courting her, and we spent a good deal of time together, including some late hours in my office. Eventually we were married. For a wedding present, the women of the office gave us a lovely drawing by Picasso, one of those nude figures that he did with three or four strokes of the pen, which Jacqui had obtained for us through her father.

But this is supposed to be about James Laughlin, not about H. Carruth.

◇◇◇

Jas was a womanizer. Everyone knew it, including the women themselves. That's an ugly word, *womanizer*, both semantically and phonetically, but it's the word that is current today, it's the word we must use if we're to be honest with ourselves. And honesty, as Jas said, is the basis of good writing.

Was the *trobador*[29] who made verses for his lady in Uzès or Tarrasson in the eleventh century a womanizer? The answer is yes, and the further answer is that we must acknowledge this if we are to keep ourselves straight with history at all. At the same time we must acknowledge also that poets live and write in the circumstances in which they find themselves, and from those circumstances they make beauty, poignance, and meaning – our whole cultural fabric.

It's a question of keeping a number of balls in the air at the same time, all these acknowledgments, and no one ever said it was easy.

Jas called his women "little birds." He would say, for instance, in a letter or a conversation, "Well, I had this little bird who lived in Lausanne – or Nantucket or Kyoto or wherever – and we dallied together for a while with much pleasure."

The prospect is, I must say, alluring, I think to everyone.

I know, because some of them told me, that Jas didn't force his attentions on any woman. After all, he was tall, handsome, charming, and rich: he didn't need to. I believe further that in most cases the woman made the first move, as Ann did, or at least that the woman and man were thrown together in a condition which was mutually and greatly agreeable. Romance is a fact of life. Jas throve on it and relished it, without doubt, and

29. The spelling in *lo lenga d'òc*, which I prefer.

made a large body of verse about it, verse which has, granted, a certain quaintness in its tone, a certain piquancy from another age, so that it seems to some readers anachronistic, not to say antiquated and passé. But a poet in the present age, or in any age, may assimilate himself if he chooses to do so to the past, to that *trobador* singing in the garden of the chateau in Périgord, who was precisely classical. Everything in Jas's early life – his family background, his education, his emerging artistic tastes and ambitions – led him to do just that.

How much do I know about the little birds? In truth I have no idea. Bits of erotic history turn up from time to time that still astonish me. But the whole notion of scandal is repugnant to me. Altogether repulsive. Over the years I learned a good deal about Jas and his little birds, but what part this may be of the whole is unknown to me, and in any case I have no intention of exploiting it. What I do know is that these women were many and came from many places, many backgrounds, many classes, and that none of them has complained, at least not in a combative way. They know about each other. They know what sexual infidelity means exactly. No doubt the patience of many of them has been sorely tried. To say nothing of the patience of their husbands and other lovers.

I know a number of these women. They are, each in her own way, darlings. I am very fond of them. Make no mistake, they are women of sensitivity, distinction, and independence. A number of them are writers and artists.

At the same time I know Jas behaved cruelly, thoughtlessly, on some occasions. He left one bed for another very abruptly and without explanation. I find this inexcusable. It is part of the "hard streak" in Jas, which made him do disgraceful, ugly things in his private life and made him obnoxious to some people. If, as I think, this was in reality a kind of "soft streak," a weakness of personality that he tried to overcome by self-manipulative toughness, does this change anything? No, nothing at all.

More and more I brood upon the conundrum of what it means to be appalled by one's steadfast friends. Less and less do I find an answer to it. The only compensation is that one is equally appalled, if not more, by oneself.

Jas also referred to his paramours as *apsaras*, which in Hindu culture are divine nymphs who fly here and there to bring delight and inspiration to mortal men.

Gertrude believes that this aspect of Jas's behavior, his womanizing, derives from his father, but because of her illness I haven't been able to explore this notion with her in detail, and I know little about Laughlin Senior. He is a shadowy figure in my mind. I do know that when Jas was a boy his father took him on visits to mistresses in London and Paris, exciting visits during which they lived in the best hotels, went to the races at Deauville, had dinner at Maxim's, etc. Jas enjoyed these excursions, he apparently enjoyed especially the camaraderie with his father. But he never said much to me about them. I naturally presume that the father was a playboy, but maybe this is an unfair exaggeration; perhaps Laughlin Senior was faithfully attending to his duties at the steel corporation in Pittsburgh most of the time. Nevertheless, Gertrude's implication that the father's behavior rubbed off on the son is worth taking into account, though I myself tend to think something more profound than that must be at the heart of the matter. Jas sought release from his repressed anxieties in sex and in sexual dominance. This is a crude and clinical way to put it because it suggests insincerity. If I know anything about Jas's poetry – and I do – it is that his love poems are utterly sincere. He had no ulterior need to write them.

What do I mean by this? Every writer has an ulterior need to write. Otherwise writers would be shoe clerks and car thieves like the rest of the population. But I do not believe this necessarily militates against substantial sincerity. The relationship between a writer's topic and his need to write is as variable and complex as any human relationship can be.

But aside from such abstruse conjectures, the plain fact is that where the little birds were concerned Jas was like a bird feeder. They flocked to him. I've just heard,[30] thirdhand, about a skiing trip that Jas and a few other young skiers made to New Zealand in the mid-'30s, probably the first time Americans had taken to the slopes in that country. The main thing everyone remembers from the journey is how the little birds of New Zealand fluttered and preened and beckoned whenever Jas was proximate. To the rest of us this may seem both mysterious and unfair, but there it is.

◇◇◇

The circle of friends and acquaintances around Jas was enormous. It wasn't one circle, in fact, but many. It was worldwide, and the people in one circle were not necessarily known to those in another. Practically speaking, I myself was outside all the circles, looking in, catching glimpses of exotic and exalted people in the distance, people at the other end of the dim corridor in a foreign hotel. One such circle, which is paradigmatic of the others, was in Chicago, which meant that I knew slightly more about it than I did about most of the rest.

New Directions had published four charming little novels by Maude Hutchins in the late 1940s and 1950s. Her husband was

30. From my friend Philip Booth, who had it from David Bradley, who was a member of the expedition.

Robert Hutchins, the wunderkind of intellectual life in America at midcentury, a philosopher of education who became the chancellor of the University of Chicago when he was still a young man. He was chancellor when I was a graduate student. I met him a couple of times but only briefly, and we were not friends, though I considered him then – and I still do – far and away the best university administrator our nation has ever known. He changed the university from an ordinary school into an educational center so large and complex that it truly did have a claim to universality. It was said that a person could go from kindergarten to the doctorate entirely within the Chicago regimen, and I believe this was true. This didn't mean much in itself, but at the same time an extraordinary assemblage of scholars and artists collected around the university at the invitation, directly or indirectly, of Hutchins, including many refugee scholars who had fled from Europe during the years of Nazi terror.

Through Maude and Bob Hutchins, Jas met many of those who were associated with the university, with the Great Books Program, the revised *Encyclopaedia Britannica*, and later the institute for democratic studies that Hutchins established in Santa Barbara (after the trustees in Chicago had tired of his reformist zeal and fired him). I have in mind such people as Jacques Maritain, Elisabeth Borgese and her husband, Ping Ferry, Adler, and others.[31]

Probably it was through this group that Jas met Charles Hoffman and others who were connected with the new Ford Foundation in those years after the war, resulting in the establishment of Intercultural Publications and my own move from Chicago, where I had known many of these people too, to New York.

31. I could, I should, check these and other names for spelling and to get their complete forms. Forgive me. I am old and my health is not great.

This was one circle, a relatively small one; also a conservative one, implicated in the Catholic revivalism of the 1950s. Many fashionable conversions among writers and artists occurred in those years: Lowell, Tate, Isabella Gardner, etc. Other circles of the Friends-of-Jas were larger, more radical, scattered over the face of the globe. They included pretty nearly the entire range of intellectual life at that time, although by 1950 the hard-core Stalinists had been eliminated. A fair number of these people wanted to spend time with Jas. Some, of course, were pests and cranks, against whom he had to protect himself when he was in New York. But others were people whom he wanted to know better, and many of these were invited to Meadow House. It wasn't at all unusual to have two, three, or four visitors at once, strangers to one another. Jas presided with his usual good-natured reserve, and everyone had a good time, with swimming in the summer, skiing in the winter, and wonderful dinners at all seasons, provided by Wonza, Mahalia, and the others in the kitchen.

I met some of these people, the ones who Jas thought might have any interest in me, I suppose. Some of the meetings were chancy and awkward. I remember one time in winter when Jas and Kenneth Rexroth were on skis, standing in the space behind the cottage and in front of the carriage house, ready to head off into the woods. I went out. Jas introduced me. Rexroth looked at me under lowering brows and said nothing. Not long before then I had copyedited the manuscript of one of his books of essays and had found a number of fundamental errors in it, for which he did not thank me. In a letter to Jas he referred to me as a "vaticide" – a verbatim quote – and as far as I'm concerned that's all anyone needs to know about Rexroth the person.

Another guest was Heinz Henghes, the German or Austrian painter whom Jas had met through Pound and who made the colophon for New Directions, the horse rising from the sea.

Henghes was an interesting guy. He wanted to visit the widow of Yves Tanguy, who lived in my old hometown, Woodbury, in a farmhouse she and her husband had renovated. He asked me to take him. We drove down to Woodbury and found the house; it was located in the part of town we used to call Hotchkissville when I was a kid. A wonderful house. It was an eighteenth-century New England saltbox with the usual components, small-paned windows, iron door-latches, a big fireplace. It had been decorated by Tanguy himself, and his widow kept it as he left it. In the main room as one entered was a billiard table set in the middle, and in the middle of the billiard table was a hand (a glover's replica), and in the middle of the hand was a delicately colored porcelain egg. On one wall was a collection of kachina dolls. On a small table was a golden mousetrap. The whole house, or what I saw of it, was similarly embellished with suggestive emblems. The widow, who was a good-looking woman of about fifty with long dark hair and who spoke English with a charming accent, received us cordially, and she and Henghes talked for a while. Then we drove back to Norfolk. It was an entertaining day for me, both the visit and the drive.

Another visitor was an Indian painter whose name was Krishen Khanna, someone Jas had met on one of his Asian expeditions. He was a small, quiet man with a pleasant way of speaking. Jas organized a painting party. We all went over to Robin Hill, which was unoccupied then, and set up a workshop in the big room overlooking the gardens. Jas and the painter were there, I was there, I think Ann was there, and some other people too, about half a dozen of us. We set up easels and worktables. I remember Jas became fascinated with making a large monochrome canvas in a particular shade of darkish lavender, and he spent a long time patiently mixing the pigments until he got just what he wanted. This was before minimalism, or at least before I was aware of it. The Indian painter, Krishen, warmed up his hand and imagination, I remember, by drawing totem poles with charcoal or a crayon in his sketchbook, fantastical things, I enjoyed watching him do them, and then he went on to do something in oils, a richly colored red-and-brown canvas. What I did escapes me. But we had a good time, it was a splendid afternoon. Granted, Robin Hill suffered a little from spilt paint, which was no doubt cleaned up by Theodore or someone else the following day.

Robin Hill stood vacant and largely unused for several years after Aunt Leila's death. Then Jas told me he wanted to sell the place. This was after I had moved away from Norfolk, and I was rather surprised by his decision; I would have thought that family sentiment would cause him to hang onto it. But I should have known better. Practical considerations supervened. Moreover, in spite of his affection for Aunt Leila – or because of it? – Jas didn't want to live in her house; he could just as well have sold Meadow House and moved into Robin Hill himself. He talked about wanting to sell the place to a private school or some other such modest institution, but this never worked out. Eventually it was sold to a wealthy man from New York.

There were other visitors. I remember Mary de Rachewiltz's son, who was an arrogant and dislikable young man if I ever met one. Hugh Kenner, Harry Levin, Edward Dahlberg. A shadowy company in my mind. Most of the visitors were unknown to me. Bob MacGregor was there from time to time, and he was a good friend and an interesting guy. Obviously Jas relied on him heavily for the management of New Directions, both editorial and administrative. Eventually Jas and Bob formed a partnership; I don't understand the exact legal significance of this, though I know Jas was well pleased, glad to be able to share some of the responsibility he had carried on his own shoulders for twenty years, and I also know how seriously upset he was a few years later when Bob died unexpectedly. Another visitor was Jas's brother from Philadelphia, a person I never had heard about. I met him abruptly one morning when I went up to Meadow House and he opened the door for me. He was a handsome man, looking suave and debonair, wearing a colorful silk dressing gown and a silk scarf around his neck, but he had an enormous, hideous scar on his forehead. I thought he must have been in an car crash, but Jas told me the scar came from boyhood when their mother had taken his brother to an incompetent radiologist for the removal of some kind of imperfection of the skin.

Was I a good friend, or was I a good servant? I never knew. I never knew if I should knock or just walk in when I went up to Meadow House. Once when I didn't knock I found Ann and her children in the dining room, getting ready to go skiing. Ann had on her long johns. At first when I came in she gave a little shriek, but then looked down at herself and said quickly, "It's all right. It's all right. I'm decent." The truth is I wouldn't have noticed her underwear if she hadn't drawn attention to it. What's the difference, essentially, between long johns and ski pants?

The visitor I remember most clearly was Ann's sister, Helen Hauge, along with her husband, Gabe, and their rather large assortment of children. Helen was a beautiful woman with prematurely snow-white hair. After Rose Marie and I were married, she continued to take an interest in Rose Marie, and was kind and friendly. But of course she was more than a visitor. Both summers when I was in Norfolk the Hauges occupied the camp all summer long. It was a beautiful site, rocky, high, overlooking the Blackberry valley, with great copses of mountain laurel all around. The drawback was the adders – the American kind, harmless but bold. They came into the house.

One time before Rose Marie and I were married, I was at the camp when she picked up a brass table lamp to mop up some spilled lemonade, and an adder was coiled in the base of it. Helen tolerated the adders with remarkable equanimity.

Somehow I ended up with a mahogany cigar humidor that had belonged to Gabe and had "Gabriel" incised on the lid. He was not a smoker. No doubt the humidor was a Christmas present from some supplier to the banking trade. A few years later Gabe developed cancer of the eye, and one of his eyes was removed. He was a not unkindly man who nevertheless always seemed preoccupied, as I suppose he was.

◇◇◇

The will has been probated. Jas has left me $5,000. I figure this means he still owes me about $100,000. But then – the poor are always the creditors of the rich, isn't that so? Generally speaking, I deplore it. But in the present case I don't much mind.

It goes without saying, though it has been said many times and I don't object to saying it again – I am *glad* to say it again – that the poor, especially the literate poor, are deeply in debt to James Laughlin in a number of other ways.

And it is essential, absolutely essential, to remember that in our minds – as in the minds of the other serious people Jas and I knew during the time of our youth – the production and publication of serious writing was not, distinctly not, a commercial endeavor. Real writers worked freely with and for one another.

◇◇◇

Joe-Anne, my wife, tells me that too many of my sentences begin with *but*. Well, how else is a writer afflicted by that great adversary, Radical Ambivalence, to proceed? Every sentence he writes contradicts the one he wrote before it.

A balance is achieved, some say. But in my observation a seesaw can never be balanced.

◇◇◇

I just spoke with Gertrude.[32] She has friends with her, friends from her life before marriage, as well as nurses. She is either in bed or in the chair next to the bed. She has a walker but doesn't use it. A couple of days ago she asked her doctor to send her "home to Jesus," but he wouldn't. She says I am the only person she will talk to.

What a misery! We swore undying love to each other, as we do in this peculiar, old peoples', morbid flirtation we carry on. Just then the nurse came in and said Gertrude must go outdoors for a while. It's a warm sunny day. Fortunately Jas installed one of those one-person, sit-down elevators on the main stairway of Meadow House several years ago. It amused him to sit on it and make it go. He called it "ascending into the next circle" as he disappeared into the hole in the ceiling. Now I'm sure it is helpful – extremely helpful, in fact – in bringing Gertrude downstairs. The whole business brings tears to my eyes.

◇◇◇

My first summer in Norfolk was the summer when everyone was talking about polio, i.e., poliomyelitis, the acute viral disease that crippled so many children, though adults were vulnerable too. In those days we all had a friend or relative with a

32. March 30, 1998.

bent leg or withered arm. We all had continually before us the memory of President Roosevelt, that good, intelligent man whose voice was a consolation to us on the radio in troubling times. We were well aware that we never saw a picture of him standing up. He couldn't. A year or two before that summer of 1960 the vaccine against polio had been announced, and during the summer it was distributed for the first time on a wide scale. I remember standing in line somewhere in the village, perhaps on the green or on the lawn in front of the library, where long tables had been set up, staffed by white-clad nurses. I was given a sugar cube instilled with a reddish, cherry-flavored liquid, and told to eat it, which I did. No more polio. What a momentous occasion in the history of our world! Yet at the time, like most healthy forty-year-olds, I don't think I paid much attention to it.

Of course the virus can and does mutate and produce ever more resistant strains. But we didn't know that then. The whole business of genetics and the double helix was still to come, though in school we had learned about what was called "eugenics" and how if you crossed a black dog and a white dog you would get two black, two white, and four spotted. Hah! The fact is that when it came to the mysteries of human essence we were like savages who have taken the back off a watch and have no idea of what the hell they are looking at.

A few weeks later I woke up one morning in the cottage with double vision, what I later learned to call vertical diplopea: my eyes were discoordinated and could not focus on the same point in a vertical plane. I felt quite ill. I called Dr. Barstow, and he came to see me soon afterward. Then he called Ann and told her that I had to be put to bed right away and kept there. Of course she volunteered the guest room at Meadow House, that's the way she was – otherwise I'd have had to go to the hospital in Winsted or Torrington. I was transported up the hill. Ann was concerned and cordial, as always, but she stayed noticeably distant from me, and I could see easily enough how anxious she was. No one wanted polio in the house, especially in a house that contained two small children.

Dr. Barstow did his best to convince her that I didn't have polio. On the other hand he didn't know what was the matter with me. He went away and did some research, and finally he called to announce that I was infected with Coxsackie virus. A little-known virus at that time, named after the town in New York where it had first appeared among the convicts in a state penitentiary. I don't know if Dr. Barstow told Ann that the Coxsackie virus and the polio virus are closely related. Maybe he kept that to himself.

I took the medicine he prescribed, stayed in bed, and slept most of the time, which wasn't difficult because I had a fever and felt groggy and disoriented. This continued for the better part of a week. Then I began to recover, my vision returned to normal, I spent a day sitting in the living room, reading and writing, and eventually I went home to the cottage.

Dr. Barstow was probably the most popular person in Norfolk. Everyone liked him and depended on him. He was kindly, friendly, humorous, but had a flinty edge to him too, a New Englander's toughness and intelligence. He was the last doctor who ever came to see me at my home. He had a house in the village, just off the green, in which a front room was his office; if you phoned and he wasn't there his wife answered. And if you made it clear that you couldn't go to his office, he took your word for it, and climbed in his car and came to see you, with his black satchel full of pills and instruments. The second summer I was in Norfolk I came down with a "bad back," a partially lapsed or dislocated sacroiliac that Dr. Barstow traced to an injury I had suffered in the army in 1943. At times it was extremely painful. Dr. Barstow came to the cottage, gave me pills, explained in detail what had happened to me, and then gave me a short course in how to live with a twinging back; he even showed me how to get in and out of bed or in and out of my car without bending or twisting.

Since then every doctor I've had has been located in a shopping mall or "professional building," surrounded by nurses, technicians, and secretaries and unavailable much of the time. When I've needed medical attention at night or on the weekend, I've gone to the emergency room of the nearest hospital, like anyone else – an expensive and supremely disagreeable hassle. And some Americans, I believe, still think we are making progress.

The guest room at Meadow House is on the first floor at one end of the house, next to but well separated from the living room. It has an attached bathroom, and is furnished with two four-posters of a colonial design that probably has a name, though who knows what it is? The beds were extraordinarily high. When I've been sleeping there – many times in the past forty years – I've always felt as if I'm too far off the ground. The room has a sofa too, an easy chair, a desk, a bureau, other chairs, etc. The bedside tables are always provided with art books, eighteenth-century diaries, the erotic poetry of Afghanistan, all kinds of literary curiosities. Also dictionaries. Large windows are on two sides, and have the distinction of being the only windows I've ever seen with blinds that pull up instead of down. They work with little pulleys so that you can close off the bottom half of the window but leave the top open to the daylight, a very sensible arrangement.

Hundreds and hundreds of people have stayed in that room. Trying to sleep or maybe trying to stay awake. Trying to figure out just what in the hell they are doing in such a place. I bet it's one of the best-known private rooms in America.

I think of William Carlos Williams lying in one of those high beds. The light from the bedside lamp glints on his glasses. He cranes his neck. He studies the patterns of cracked paint on the ceiling, where you can see a charging lion if you look carefully enough. At last he sighs, removes his glasses, switches off the light, turns his back to the other, empty bed, and goes to sleep.

By the fence which separates the yard from the meadow – a fence made of cedar poles – a shadblow tree grows. A slight tree of a vaguely oriental cast. You've seen it on a number of Japanese screens. In spring, at the time when the shad are running in the Hudson, it flowers with a delicate white bloom, very beautiful, which is why it is called shadblow or shadbush (*Amelanchier canadensis*). In other regions it is called service-berry or Juneberry. Jas was particularly fond of that little tree, and he told me that Williams, who had been visiting once when it was in bloom, had been much taken with it too. I can imagine the good doctor-poet looking at it intently.

Once when the tree was badly damaged in an ice storm it was replaced with another well-grown shadblow sapling as soon as springtime came.

I never saw Jas in the guest room, not once in all the years. I don't know what to make of this especially, except that Jas was the kind of a man who is willing to stay out of parts of his own house.

◇◇◇

Jas was as granitic a Yankee son of William James as anyone I've ever known, and certainly he was dependent on his posses-sions: his car, his Dictaphone, his typewriter, and eyeglasses. Yet I never heard him express the least attachment to a tool or artifact, not even a particular set of ski poles or a long-used overcoat. He seemed not to care about such things, to be distant from them, utterly impersonal. He used whatever lay easily at hand.

His only material loves were books and paintings.

From time to time one was reminded, however, that the Yankee pragmatist was fascinated by Asian philosophy and religion. Not that he ever said anything unironical about them, or about anything else, but rather that he moved through the world with a kind of unaffected detachment, not serene, not sprightly, not anything – just detached.

Jas favored the Hindu rather than the Taoist or Zen strain of Asian culture, I think. He was a sensualist. A spiritual sensualist. Sometimes he fancied himself as Krishna.

What about music? I never heard him sing, or even hum or whistle. I have the impression he was tone-deaf, couldn't carry a tune, though I'm not sure why I have it. I just assume, I suppose, that anyone who never makes music at all cannot make it. But Jas was fond of music, he listened to it a lot. He had an elaborate stereo system set on a landing just off the living room, near his desk. When he found a record he liked, he would play it again and again. I remember a record of Kathleen Ferrier, the wonderful Canadian contralto, singing against an accompaniment of cello and harp. For a while, perhaps several weeks, he played it almost constantly. Granted, he worked while he listened, but you could tell he was really hearing and relishing the sound, especially certain passages that touched him deeply. He would look up and stare out the window without moving. He was like an adolescent who listens to the Stones while doing an assignment for school.

Even so, he had no sentimental feeling for his stereo. If it failed to work properly, he wasn't even annoyed. He shrugged and turned to something else.

◇◇◇

At some point in the early or middle 1980s a tribute was orga-
nized for Jas and celebrated in an auditorium somewhere in
New York, perhaps at Cooper Union. I was there along with a
few hundred other people. A number of us spoke. We paraded
to the podium and said what we wanted to say while Jas sat
behind us on the stage, half obscured in shadow. When the
master of ceremonies – George Plimpton or Robert Giroux or
somebody like that – introduced me, Jas boomed out the only
words he uttered on stage that evening, except for his statement
of thanks at the end: "Hayden is a rock, an absolute rock." I was
astonished. No one ever felt more unrocklike than I, then and
always. Was that how he perceived me?

Maybe it was.

Afterward there was a party at Drue Heinz's splendid house
on the east side.

Gertrude was in the audience that night. We hadn't seen
each other since the days of Intercultural, twenty-five years ear-
lier. After the ceremonies concluded we embraced, and I said,
"Oh, Gertrude, it's good to see you. It's been a fucking long time."
Well, I'm known as the most profane man in Madison County,
New York, but Gertrude didn't mind. She hugged me and
kissed my beardy cheek. Ever since then, in letters to me and
conversations, she has been at pains to sprinkle her speech
with plenty of four-letter words, and she does it joyfully, as-
sertively, as if it were a kind of release for her. Perhaps it was.
God knows, Jas took her to too many solemn literary occasions
in too many pretentious houses in the old days – he had to. No
one was ever quicker than Gertrude to scorn solemnity and
pretension, at least in private.

During the long interregnum, Gertrude and I had been in

touch once or twice. One summer I received a letter from her postmarked somewhere on the northern shore of the St. Lawrence estuary in Québec, downstream from Québec City where the river becomes very broad. I've never been in that part of Canada, even though I lived not far away in northern Vermont. But I liked to imagine Gertrude having a long cool drink at a table on some esplanade overlooking the river in radiant Canadian summer sunshine, blonde, blue-eyed, and smiling. Talking French. A painting by Renoir.

◇◇◇

Maybe, on the other hand, when Jas called me a "rock" in public, he knew exactly how unrocklike I felt, and he was trying to encourage me and make me feel better.

Kindness was always – I do not exaggerate – a spontaneous impulse in the conduct of Jas Laughlin, but many people could not recognize this because kindness was also always an impulse he spontaneously recoiled from and distrusted and disguised.

> There was a crooked man
>   Who went a crooked mile
> And found a crooked sixpence
>   Beside a crooked stile.
>
> He bought a crooked cat
>   That caught a crooked mouse
> And they all lived together
>   In a little crooked house.

◇◇◇

Like many people of both genders who are conspicuously motivated by sex, Jas was obsessed by the idea of personal extinction. He was terrorized by it. He thought about death a lot and wrote about it frequently. In his speech he made many wry allusions to it. On the other hand he never made any straightforward statement about death to me, and I doubt that he did to anyone else either, unless it was his shrink. Being Jas's shrink would have been an unenviable job.

And Jas always had something wrong with him to complain about. When I first met him it was his sinus. He carried a Benzedrine inhaler with him at all times and took frequent sniffs. When he was skiing, he stopped often to use it. He blew his nose. He pressed his hands against his cheekbones. He complained. Eventually he had an operation to relieve the pressure, and it helped him a good deal.

Then came the whole episode with depression, lithium, and the shrink. He did not complain about this openly, but his letters made frequent half-veiled reference to his headshrinking and the witch doctor.

Later, in his sixties and seventies, he complained about arthritis. Often I found him lying on the sofa in the living room at Meadow House, wearing one of those high, uncomfortable-looking collars to prop up his neck. He would say that he couldn't move, that he was as bound up as a trussed hog. But he continued to work, to run the typewriter, to figure out the royalties – and to write his poems.

As old age came upon him Jas appeared more and more feeble. He would shuffle and stagger when he walked, he would hang onto chairs and tables to keep his balance. He would take three minutes to get up from his chair, and if there was a handy gripping post nearby, like a door frame or a bookcase, he would grasp it with both hands and haul himself up shakily.

Gertrude said this was affectation, at least in part, done to attract sympathy; she said she saw him get up without difficulty when he thought he was unobserved. I don't dispute her. She was living with him and she ought to know. But I must say at the same time that Jas's pain and infirmity seemed quite genuine to me, not faked at all, perhaps because I was getting to the age at which I felt them myself. Or perhaps Gertrude was right and Jas was just a very good actor.

Whatever the case may have been, the last year or two were painful for me to observe. Jas carried on. Time after time my mail contained new poems that astonished me; he was more and more prolific as time passed, it seemed, and though he wrote some clunkers, as we all do, his new work was often remarkably original and acute. I found this astonishing because in my own mind, after I passed seventy-five, the loss of mental energy was manifest and troubling. Every day Jas went for a walk unless it was pouring. He would go into the woods with his attendant, a Hungarian man named Sandor, to guide him, hold back the infringing branches of the trees, and help him up if he fell; he would follow the old ski trails through the pines and spruces, walking slowly but doggedly, looking at every familiar thing, left and right. When I went with him I walked behind him, just as I had always skied behind him in the old days, and this inspired him to write a poem about "the man who walks behind me." Jas turned almost everything into poetry. His mind was always working poetically.

Toward the end I saw little intimations that Jas was succumbing more and more to his internal terrors. Nothing explicit, just little glances and gestures, little lip-tremors and rapid eye-blinks, which were unmistakable to any friend who knew him well. At times he was afflicted with momentary hallucinations – voices and shadows. The schizoid quality of experience – for he had always pictured himself in a double perspective – became more pronounced.

When he died I was not in Norfolk. At that time I was having serious difficulties in my own personal life. Apparently his doctor – I don't know which one, but it might have been Nason Hamlin, who is the general practititoner in Norfolk now, Dr. Barstow's successor whom everyone admires and who took care of Jas and Gertrude – ordered Jas to have an MRI exam at the hospital in Torrington. I don't know the details. Jas had been tentatively diagnosed with "super nuclear palsy," related to Parkinson's, which gives the patient great difficulty with swallowing and speaking. I saw the first symptoms of this when I visited in the summer of 1997. At any rate Jas found himself inside that polished steel tube with outrageous loud noises banging in his ears, and he was terrified. He lost his mind, I think literally, though whether or not he had a stroke, as was announced to the press by New Directions, is problematical. The time in the hospital was unspeakably awful; so I've been told. I talked with Gertrude, who was very ill too, on the phone almost every day. After a week or so Jas was brought home to Meadow House. I suggested to Gertrude that I could drive over to Norfolk and say hello to him. "He might recognize you," Gertrude said, "but probably not." I asked her if she thought he could ever return to anything resembling his former life, and she said flatly, no.

Her next phone call was to announce his death, two days after his return to Meadow House. But it was some time before I realized how extraordinarily ill and miserable he had been during his final days. The super nuclear palsy was a nightmare.

That moment inside the polished steel tube stays in my mind. It's like an image from a story by Kafka, absolutely central and controlling in my life.

James Laughlin,
Norfolk, 1993.

Hayden Carruth,
New York City, 1992.

◇◇◇

After I left Norfolk my relationship with Ann became naturally less substantial, so to speak. When I visited Norfolk we were always exuberantly friendly; she "made a fuss" over me, and over Rose Marie and the Bo, too. But the rest of the time we did not communicate regularly. Letters and phone calls now and then, but nothing at all intensive. I was in close touch with Jas, after all, and he gave me the family news. Ann communicated with me rarely, and when she did it was usually about the Bo.

She was his godmother. She took a godmotherly interest in him and his welfare. She established a savings account for him at a bank in Stamford or New Canaan, which is where she came from. At Christmas she sent him a little check.

The whole business of godparenting seemed to me a sentimental absurdity, like everything else connected with Christian convention, but I went along with it anyway, which is as good an indication as any of my passivity in the face of Laughlinesque precedence. The christening was performed at the church in Norfolk, which was a characteristic New England Protestant church, built with white clapboards, clear glass windows, a steeple, oaken pews, a good-enough organ, etc. My brother David, for whom the Bo was named, served as godfather. I can't remember for certain if Jas was there, but I don't think he was. Myself, I stood in the background, mumbled the necessary responses, and let Ann and David and the minister do what they did. This was what was expected, in the family and in the town, and this is what we did.

What did Christianity mean to Jas? I think I know, but as usual I'm not certain. Jas supported the church with annual contributions, he was on friendly terms with the pastor, during much of his life he attended services on Christmas, Easter, and a few other holy days. In his ordinary speech – and to some extent in his poems and other writings – he occasionally uttered pious sentiments, though in a wry, "knowing" way. Did these utterances have any religious significance at all? I think not. That's my inference, perhaps my supposition – but I don't know for sure.

During his final terror did Jas receive any help or succor from faith? Again I think not.

To the extent that Jas believed anything, outside a few fundamental esthetic propositions, he believed in the efficacy of forms. He was like T.S. Eliot in this respect. But whereas Eliot would have said that observing the letter of the law was ultimately useless without observing the spirit of the law as well, Jas put his faith, a very limited faith, in the observance of the letter alone. Codes of conduct were at least somewhat important to him. If one observed them most of the time one helped to protect the ordinary social fabric, the life of the town. Going to church once in a while was like saying good morning to one's neighbors at the post office even though one rarely spoke to them at any other time. The social fabric was a tissue of ethical amenities, sufficiently bland to hold together ordinary people who otherwise had no interest in each other. This was the fabric against which – or within which or in combination with which – the arts could flourish.

Ann had a "back problem." It bothered her a good deal at times, though she didn't complain. One day I received a letter from Jas in which he said that her difficulty had finally been diagnosed as spinal cancer and that she was in the hospital. A sequence of treatments ensued, in a series of hospitals, over a somewhat protracted time, during which I never saw Ann or heard directly from her. Eventually she came home to Meadow House, and it was understood that she came home to die.

During this time Jas wrote to me in bleak and bitter terms. The pious allusions continued, but the tone of his feeling was more existential than Christian. He was a man of the twentieth century, after all, who had read Sartre and Camus and probably Husserl and Heidegger. He had also read Martin Buber. He had read many, many books, and his view was befittingly complex. He could utter the pieties in the same spirit that Paul Goodman did,[33] and at the same time confront face-to-face the brutality of existence.

Jas attended Ann faithfully. It was his duty to subject himself to the horror of helping his wife to die, and he did it – responsibly and with a kind of wrenching concern. He reported this to me sketchily in his letters – the nursing, the arrangements, the daily routines. He stayed with her and talked with her, as he had with Aunt Leila. It would be extremely enlightening to know what those conversations touched on. We don't, and almost certainly we never will.[34] In his letters he excoriated pain and death while at the same time he submitted to them, but less in the spirit of acceptance than in the spirit of resistant disacquiescence. And I do not for a moment – I emphasize this – I do not for a moment suggest that a profound and perfectly sincere affection for Ann was not uppermost in his feelings during that time.

In her will Ann left a bequest of $5,000 to the Bo. It was a long time before her estate was settled and he received his check, but when it came it helped a good deal with his college expenses, which is what Ann wanted.

Not long after Ann's death Jas escaped from what had been

33. Cf. *Little Prayers and Finite Experience*.
34. Nevertheless some who should know say that Ann became fed up with Jas and his ways at the end. Their conversations may have been less amicable, at least on her part, than I have suggested. Others who attended her faithfully during her illness were her sister, Helen Hauge, and her stepdaughter, Leila Javitch.

the confinement of Meadow House during her illness. He turned, returned, to Gertude. Before long they were married and she moved into Meadow House. One night she and I were sitting at the dinner table after Jas had left to write some letters or read Aubrey's *Brief Lives* or whatever he was doing that evening. Gertrude and I were sipping champagne. She showed me a special bottle cap she had with which she could close an opened bottle of sparkling wine and keep it fresh; later she gave me one like it. She said, "For forty years this was what I most wanted." She made a circling gesture with her finger to indicate the whole ambience of the house and her marriage. "How could I have been so wrong?" The starkness of her revelation was undeniable, but she knew that I would understand. I did. Because I don't, and can't, believe in absolute admiration – or any absolute at all – I could acknowledge my understanding of Gertrude's plight without altering my feeling about Jas. As she herself could too, although more in the mode of Christian charity and forbearance than in my way of acceding to the un-analyzable complexities of human personality. I record this episode in full awareness of the fact that many people will re-gard it as a breach of decorum. It isn't a breach of confidence, however; if I thought it were I'd leave it out. As for decorum, it has less importance for me than it had for Jas. Yet he himself was delighted by breaches of decorum, especially if they oc-curred in the eighteenth century or earlier.

Ann was a lost soul. I always felt that. With her forced cheerfulness and managerial eagerness, she sought to over-come all the obvious shortcomings of her life, including the ones that she felt derived from her own nature. It was a perpet-ually failing effort, perpetually renewed. Her energy, until ill-ness laid her flat, was boundless. But I confess that my love for her was in a large part pity.

As he grew older Jas became more and more ambitious for his own work, as if he desired more and more ardently to refute the unkind judgment Ez had laid on him back in 1935. I don't know when the turning point was, or if any turning point occurred at all, but clearly he changed, during the 1980s, from being extremely reticent about his poetry to being eager and enterprising about it. Perhaps the turning point was the publication of his *Selected Poems 1935–1985* by Larry Ferlinghetti at City Lights in 1986. This was a considerable upgrade from his earlier books, a substantial hardcover volume with notes, an index, a brief foreword by Marjorie Perloff, the whole designed by Gertrude and printed at an unspecified but obviously first-rate commercial printery, probably chosen by Jas. The book sold for $25.95. On the flyleaf of my copy Jas wrote: "For Hayden…" followed characteristically by three words of Greek that I can't read, and then signed "Jas." He had adopted my version of his name.[35] I should get someone to translate the Greek for me. It's probably a quotation and probably flattering – that is, if he wasn't in a whimsical mood when he wrote it.

Or perhaps the turning point was a few years earlier when Jas wrote the poem called "In Another Country," which was a poem of formidable proportions for him, extending over several pages and mixing two languages, English and Italian. The mixture of languages was nothing new in poetry, and of course the example of Pound was always before him. But Jas wanted to

---

35. Pound used to call him "Jaz," and maybe this influenced my own decision to call him "Jas." But I don't think so. I began doing it sometime during the 1970s. People close to him in his family called him "James." He usually signed himself "J" – and that's what most friends and colleagues called him. He disliked it, however, when anyone referred to him in writing as "Jay."

go beyond Pound; he wanted to use foreign languages in his poems not as tags or tokens or fragments ripped from another context, but rather as integral narrative components of the poem, which meant either that the reader must be able to read the foreign parts of the poem or that the foreign parts must be presented in such a way that they are intelligible to the reader who cannot read them. The latter was what Jas aspired to. A very difficult technical challenge. Pound had solved it – sometimes – by offering translations of his foreign quotes within the text of the poem itself; you can see this in the *Cantos*. Eliot put translations in his notes. But Jas didn't want such trickery in his work because he felt it was precious, pedantic, too artificial. He wanted his poem to be seamless from language to language. He achieved this by using the foreign language, in this case Italian, so simply that any literate reader with a smattering of Romance languages could understand it. And when translation was indispensable, he tried to couch the translation in such a way that it seemed a natural – always his first aim – part of the discourse. This meant writing an Italian that was plain, colloquial, even a bit vulgar, but this was what he was doing in English already, and had been doing from the start. "In Another Country" was a perfect piece, if you bear these requirements in mind. He did exactly what he wanted to do. Perhaps only another writer, another language worker, can understand how gratifying that was for him.

I'm not sure when I first saw "In Another Country." Jas sent it to me in manuscript, and I made a few suggestions, not many, for improvement. This was while I was living in Vermont. I have the impression that I then published it in *Harper's*, where I was serving as poetry editor, but I may be mistaken; it would have been a long poem for publication in such a magazine. (I know I published something of his, however.) Jas himself recognized the importance of this poem, I believe, because when he published a small collection in about 1982, also with City Lights, he used "In Another Country" as the title poem.

Jas was sending me poems pretty regularly at that time. He continued to do so until the end, and in fact the envelopes got fatter and fatter. He was astonishingly prolific once he decided to make a run for it, as he might have said. Most of the poems were short, most of them incorporated classical allusions in one way or another, and most of them were erotic. "In Another Country" was a poem about an encounter in Italy with a girl who took him to a cave on the shore of Lake Como that could be reached only by swimming underwater, a cave near the cove celebrated by Catullus…

Well, I've looked up the poem, and I see I'm confusing places, and probably inventing sources. Please forgive me. The point I'm making still holds. In this poem Jas did pretty much what he wanted to do. And what he wanted to do ultimately, like most of us, was to make a poem that said more than it says. This poem about an amorous encounter between two young people is, without any internal explication whatever, nevertheless clearly paradigmatic of the perils and pleasures of intercultural exchange during a time of war and international trepidation.

As time went by, Jas wrote bigger and bigger poems. He found that the short-line poem he was used to writing, even if he didn't stick closely to the typewriter prosody he had used in the past, was still the most comfortable means for transcribing his memories into the autobiographical pieces he desired to leave behind him. He came to call these pieces "Byways," meaning that they concerned incidental excursions away from the main highway of his life, which had been New Directions. At first this was a working title only; it sounded a little quaint, a little Yeatsian. But after a while he saw that it was right, and he adopted it in earnest.

He sent me chunks of this material, and he commissioned me explicitly to revise and edit them. He was businesslike about it; this was different from the changes I made in the little poems. He would send me a check along with his request for my help and his instructions about what he wanted. Not a big check. But he wanted to pay me, and I think for two reasons: first, to help me with my somewhat precarious finances,[36] and, secondly, to assure a kind of semiprofessional relationship between us with respect to this larger work, i.e., he didn't want to impose – not ever. I was at work on pieces of his frequently during the last twenty-five years of his life.

I was amused, incidentally, by the increasing parsimony of Jas's later years. Of course he hadn't accomplished what he did by throwing his money away, but as he got older he seemed to feel the pinch – a totally imaginary pinch, as far as I know – more and more, and he even gave up smoking expensive cigars from Dunhill's or Sherman's in New York and switched to ordinary Garcia y Vegas cigars from the Norfolk Pharmacy. Once he asked me to take him down to the village. My car was a small Japanese import, but I pushed the passenger seat back as far as it would go, and he climbed in. "This is great," he said, and then he spied a cigar butt in my ashtray, "and there's even a cigar for me," he exclaimed, and snatched it up, a remnant of a dark, bitter, Connecticut-Valley cigar such as I smoked in those days. He lit up and puffed contentedly. "Not bad," he said. From Jas that was high praise. In his view Dante's *Inferno* was "not really a bad poem at all."

The last big job I did for Jas took about three months in the

36. Though my problems eased when I moved to Syracuse in 1980 and began to teach in the university there, he still wanted to pay me.

spring and early summer of 1997. He sent me a package containing several folders of manuscript, mostly in rough shape, along with letters, Xeroxed passages from source books, all kinds of things. This was his *Commonplace Book*. It consisted of quotations he had jotted down from his reading over many years, translated where necessary, arranged into Laughlinesque style, all in strophes of five lines. His pentastichs. Sometimes he called them his "fivers" or his "pents." He wanted me to make a selection of them, revise and edit them, and arrange them into proper order for a book. Which is what I did. I rewrote a fair number of the pentastichs to make them more consistent and take advantage of Jas's own style and diction, I regularized the titles and notes, I put the poems into an intentionally random but varied order, and I retyped the whole thing on my computer in order to make a manuscript that would be ready for the typesetter and easily manageable for the designer, who was Leslie Miller of The Grenfell Press in New York. She did a fine job, and the book was published – by New Directions – after Jas died. He was so pleased with the work I did for him on the book that he sent me an extra $500 for it after I returned the finished manuscript to him. This was in September or October.

When Jas and I got back from the village that day – and I believe this was during my last visit to Meadow House – we were standing in the back entry next to the kitchen when Jas dropped a box of matches on the floor. He groaned and began to stoop and immediately said, "Don't bother about them, I can get them." But I squatted down next to him anyway and helped to retrieve the matches and return them to the matchbox. A couple of days later I wrote this poem:

THE AFTERLIFE: REMEMBERING MATCHES

Once when I was an old poet and was visiting
An even older poet, he dropped a box

Of matches that scattered every which way
At our feet, and although he asked me not to,
I stooped to help him retrieve them and restore them
Neatly to their box, the red ends pointing
All in the same direction. What a delight –
One of those little moments of gratification
That St. Augustine says are the only value
In life and the presages of a divine presence.
My friend was a great man, and so in a far
Less significant way was I, and I helped him
Return his scattered matches to their little box.

It was a ridiculously easy poem to write. All I had to do was recount what had actually happened, just as it happened. The only imaginative element was the gimmick of writing in the "afterlife," but this seemed natural because by that time both Jas and I were on the brink of the grave, and we knew it. I liked this idea and went on to write several other poems as if from the beyond.

Of course then there's the question of St. Augustine. Did the good saint ever say anything like what I ascribed to him? I have no idea. From time to time Carruth has been known to make things up in his poems. I believe the same can be said of Laughlin, though when he quotes a classical text you can be sure it's accurate.

At any rate, my poem was read publicly by someone at the memorial service for Jas in New York in January, 1998, which I did not attend. Is it such an anomaly that I choose not to mourn the deaths of my good friends in public? Apparently many people think it is. But Jas would have understood.

◇◇◇

After I completed work on the *Commonplace Book,* Jas wanted me to do one more job for him, a very big job. He was desperate. Actually Gertrude was the first to approach me, and she did it on the telephone. But then a day or two afterward I received a letter from Jas that I later learned had been written with the help of his son-in-law, Daniel Javitch, and I think with other people's too. It was an uncharacteristic letter. He was frantic, and the letter revealed his anxiety. He beseeched me – his word – to take over the writing of a history of New Directions that had been commissioned from someone else; I was the only one, he said, who could do it. He offered me a large amount of money, or what seemed to me like a large amount. The manuscript that had been commissioned, a preliminary draft, had come in, and Jas found it unsatisfactory, to say the least. Actually he thought I had written the only part of the manuscript that he approved, but in fact I hadn't, I had never seen the manuscript in my life. Earlier that summer, however, I had been interviewed by the fellow who was doing the job, and apparently some of my characteristic language crept into the draft that Jas saw. Well, I reassured him; I wrote and told him the history would be written properly, New Directions would be decorously but comprehensively monumentalized; I guess I told him I would do it. But I doubt that his anxiety was much alleviated. A few days later the episode in the steel tube occurred. To what extent Jas's anxiety over his health and his immediate predicament in the tube had been augmented by his anxiety over the history, no one can say. But I believe there was a connection. How could there not be?

The anxiety over the history of New Directions had a long history itself. As I think I've already written, one of the tasks assigned to me while I was living in Norfolk was a history of the company that could be published in conjunction with a complete bibliographical list of titles published by the company from the beginning. I wrote it. I gave it to Jas and he said that although he was flattered he couldn't approve what I had done or condone its publication. Jas simply refused to believe that the history of New Directions could not be written apart from the history of James Laughlin. Yet obviously it couldn't, not if it was to be accurate in the fullest sense. His desire for a history that would leave him out was simply unrealistic.

My history was shelved, and in its place we did *A New Directions Reader*, which contained the bibliography that someone else had prepared. That was in 1964. For thirty years afterward the idea of the history continued to nag Jas and pester him. He wanted it, but he didn't want it. He was up a tree. This made him extremely uncomfortable.

My reassurances before his death were unrealistic too, as I knew very well when I offered them. I knew I couldn't do the job he wanted. I told him I would do it only because he was suffering so obviously and I was trying to help him get past a crisis. Since his death the idea of the history has been put aside, at least for the time being. I've told Daniel Javitch – and others – that I'm too old to take on such a job.

The history of New Directions could be a wonderful cultural study in the evolution of modernism in America, obviously. The two are intertwined. But it would take a person of great critical intelligence and scholarly aptitude to produce such a work, someone like Hugh Kenner or Jacques Barzun or Taylor Stoehr, and he or she would have to devote twenty years to it, or more. It would be a lifework. Whether such a person will appear is impossible to tell, but I hope so – I hope it fervently. The result could be momentous. And the material is all there, everything has been saved, the internal records, the correspondence, the whole confabulation of desires and opinions, conflicts and resolutions, and of course the erratic interventions of chance. It is an enormous, not to say panic-inducing, mass of evidence. But it could be assimilated by a mind sufficiently ambitious and talented.

◇◇◇

Once toward the end of a winter in the early 1990s my wife – that's Joe-Anne McLaughlin, the poet; we were married in 1989 – and I were visiting at Meadow House, and all of us were invited to dinner by a friend and distant neighbor of the Laughlins, a fellow who lived in a fancy house à la Wright on the Torrington road. We drove to his place. The night was nasty and turning nastier, with sleet and wet snow; the road was slippery. Gertrude, who was driving, was frightened. We reached the friend's house safely, however, went in and had drinks, then set off to a restaurant the friend recommended in Litchfield or Sharon. This time we were in the friend's Mercedes and he was driving; Gertrude and Jas were in front with him, Joe-Anne and I in the back. The friend was exuberant. He had that afternoon concluded two deals that satisfied him immensely. He had bought a mine in South America, I think Colombia – yes, he'd actually bought a mine, in case anyone thinks this happens only in movies! – and he had also bought a villa in Athens for his mother to live in. He was crowing about these coups all the way to the restaurant – not in an offensive manner, he was rather boyish in his exultation, but I was half-drunk, and I decided to be offended anyway. What the hell, nobody should have the privilege of talking like that in front of poor people. Joe-Anne and I were poking each other in the backseat, whispering together, invoking the spirits of Marx and Bakunin. When we reached the restaurant I refused to eat dinner with this guy, and although Joe-Anne tried to stop me, I went off and found a working-class bar where I had something more to drink, which wasn't necessary, and a sandwich. None of this would be worth recounting except for Jas's response to it all. When we reached home, after a slow difficult drive, I was already feeling considerably embarrassed, half-loaded though I was. Today my behavior that night seems altogether inexcusable. But all Jas said was: "Well, Hayden's a poet. He can do that kind of thing."

He said it jokingly, in his usual ironic way, but I think he more than half believed what he said. I know he did. Jas was a modernist, and much as he may have welcomed some elements of post-modernism among the Beats and the Language Poets, he was steeped in the élitist attitudes of Eliot, Pound, Wyndham Lewis, Gide, Cocteau, Gottfried Benn, and almost everyone else in the period between the two wars. We all must bow down to *l'homme – ou la femme – d'esprit.* Rexroth's vatic self-image didn't disturb Jas; that is to say, I'm sure Jas wouldn't have defended it seriously or ideologically, but as a mode of ordinary behavior in the working world of artists and writers he found it acceptable, even praiseworthy. So strong still, long after the Dadaistes, was the impulse to shock the bourgeois – *épater les bourgeoises.*

If this had ever been necessary, which I doubt, though it must have been a hell of a lot of fun at one time, certainly the necessity was long past in 1990.

At all events Jas took strongly to Joe-Anne, as well he might. She is a spectacularly good-looking, sexy woman, thirty years younger than I am, and she always makes an astonishing first impression, I've seen it time and again – and a damned fine second and third impression too, because she is charming and acutely intelligent. Jas called her my "little bird." "Be sure to bring your little bird," he would say to me when I was planning a visit.

The feeling was not reciprocated. Joe-Anne is a tough, independent-minded woman, she has had to be. She thought Jas was unbearable. In this she was totally the opposite of various other female poets I've known, who have draped themselves all over Jas in the hope of getting published. Sometimes it's worked, too.

Other friends of mine, both women and men, have shared Joe-Anne's view.

This seems to me probably rather shallow, but how can every view be deep? It isn't humanly possible. For my part, I try to refrain from judgment. No one's behavior is despicable except my own, and I believe this implicitly.

◇◇◇

Recently one of the people who have been going through Jas's papers since his death[37] has sent me a copy of a letter Jas wrote to me dated April 27, 1961. It is addressed to me in Pleasantville, not Norfolk. So one more time my memory is shown up for the bag of oatmeal it is. I had thought I was living in Norfolk on that date. The letter concerns a manuscript I had written on assignment from Jas, an introduction to a projected anthology of selections from books published by New Directions, to celebrate the twenty-fifth anniversary. Jas objected to some of the things I had written. But I have no recollection of writing that introduction, none whatever.

It means, since the introduction evidently contained information I could not have found without digging into the archives in Norfolk, that I had been in Norfolk, had visited Meadow House, for a longer period and perhaps more frequently than I realized, before I went there to live – long enough to do some serious research. In other words my work on the collection of magazines was not the only work I did in Norfolk before I moved there. Obviously I went home to Pleasantville

37. Daniel Javitch.

and wrote the introduction there. Furthermore, it probably also means I was working on my "history" of New Directions, the one that was scotched because Jas didn't like it, before I went to Norfolk. The projected anthology was never published in the form Jas anticipated. Instead it turned into the *New Directions Reader*, to which Jas himself wrote the introduction, and this came out too late to celebrate the anniversary.

All which is a good demonstration, if one were needed, that this memoir has little use as a source of data. Everything in it, every date and name and point of fact, may be wrong. One can only hope it may have other uses.

It's a further demonstration, too, of the one area in which Jas and I could not work together: I could not write about him without making him more than the shadowy, behind-the-scenes *éminence grise* he wished to be in public. My admiration and respect were too great, and his reticence was too strong. Beyond this, every day that I've worked on this memoir I've seen more clearly the extent to which Jas engineered – the word is not too forceful – the whole second half of my life, from age forty until the present. The visits to Norfolk, my residence there, the urging on to Vermont, all the jobs and commissions, the trust he placed in me: everything was done to keep me not only alive but active and at work, to keep me pushing at the borders of my limitations. All without acknowledgment, almost without thanks. But that's the way he wanted it, that's the kind of man he was, not simply in his relationship to me, but to everyone and everything.

It is well understood that Jas was personally responsible for the material survival of half a dozen brilliant and impecunious and disgraceful writers whom we can all name. More than half a dozen. But I won't name them, and I know no one else temerarious enough to do it either. Jas forbade it, simply by the sternness of his self-effacement.

Should I go back to the beginning and rewrite this memoir to make it more accurate? That is what Jas would have suggested. He was a stickler not only for accuracy but for tidiness. But this is my work, not his. I could and did mimic his style in language, though not in other things, when I needed to, but my own poetry and prose were always naturally different from his, to say the least. This is a matter of esthetic, not moral, judgment. To my mind the value of the kind of writing I'm doing here, if it has any, is in its spontaneity, its closeness to the actual mental flow, which is a virtue that Jas did not appraise highly.

I will leave this thing the way it is.

◇◇◇

The letter Jas wrote to me in April 1961 was eleven pages long and contained fifty-one numbered points of correction, amplification, and objecton. It was typed by himself on his little Royal. Marginal notes and interlineations were made by hand. Clearly the manuscript I had written, on which his letter was based, had been a substantial one. No copy of it exists, as far as I know, and I don't remember it. It's a complete blank in my mind.

When I was in the hospital, 1953 to 1955, I had been given a series of ten electroshock "treatments," which knocked out my memory of many events that occurred during the last months in New York. Did they also knock out my capacity for remembering events later on? I recall that I felt my intelligence had been distinctly, though unmeasurably, blunted by the experience. The doctors assured me that this could not be the case.

Jas's letter has been sent to me in a copy from his files. Did he have a copying machine in 1961? He must have had one. I think the early Thermofax copiers were in use at that time. Later he became fascinated with copying machines, which in effect are little printing presses, and he bought a Canon for Meadow House, with which he amused himself by making up fancy stationery with illustrations lifted from ancient texts.

◇◇◇

Time for the peroration. No doubt this writing has gone on too long already, though the work has passed quickly for me. Quickly and pleasantly. An old man doing what old men do best – remembering. Though God knows the memory grows dim. It's been a happy interlude, springing from a profoundly unhappy one: the death of a good friend. What a sorry muddle. And all of us are complicit, all of us are guilty.[38]

As the years went by and Jas became more focused on his own writing, he also became a performer on the academic circuit, which is an outcome he would have been absolutely astonished to contemplate in his youth. Ann encouraged him in this, however, and perhaps his shrink did too; it was an effective antidote for the depression. As it turned out, the universities

---

38. This work is almost done. First draft completed, revisions made. As of today, April 6, 1998, Gertude is still struggling, but she cannot talk, sleeps little, eats almost nothing, and she sometimes behaves uncharacteristically, i.e., meanly. The personality is breaking down and the cancer is running its course. In a way this was Gertrude's choice, because she decided firmly some time ago to shun surgery; she told me this last October but did not say why. I think it is connected with her feeling about the sanctity of the human body, God's creation. In any case, although I have still not spoken with a doctor, the chemo and radiation have clearly not been enough, and the end is coming soon. Maggie, a local woman from Norfolk who works in the place once occupied by Wonza and Mahalia, is Gertrude's mainstay now, a wonderfully kind and intelligent person whom I like a lot. She is the one who talks with me on the phone. We laugh and cry together. Maggie says the doctors think that Gertrude's lung cancer may have metastasized to her brain.

wanted him not only as a reader of his own work but especially as a lecturer on his experience in publishing, his personal knowledge of Pound and Williams, Stein and Miller. He worked up a number of lectures and he delivered them to eagerly interested audiences all over the country. Traveling had never been a problem for him; he was as at home on a turbojet as he was in Meadow House. He hobnobbed with young scholars and writers everywhere. "And did you see Shelley plain?" – that was the gist of their fascination. Here was a man who came from the shadowy heart of modernism even though he was still alive, a man who had listened to Pound on the sunny hillside above Rapallo, who had spoken with Eliot in his club in London, who had driven Gertrude Stein to an appointment with the hairdresser. At one point Jas became an officially listed adjunct of some kind on the faculty at Brown University, where he conducted a class in modern literature with two or three other professors. Many a time he must have heard in his mind the warnings old Ez had given him about the pitfalls of the learneries.

Jas never succumbed to the blandishments of academia, any more than he succumbed to the blandishments of the Latin Quarter or Deauville. But he enjoyed himself. He was working hard, he was doing something useful, and he was surrounded by eager neophytes, many of them young women – what could be more flattering?

He became awfully tired, however, and his arthritis became awfully painful. It was just as he had predicted for years: his skull was becoming more and more visible beneath the surface tissue when he looked in the mirror. He continued to shave himself dutifully every morning, however. He kept up his endless wry commentary, both in speech and in his mind.

And he wrote poems. Every day. Sometimes three or four a

day. And when he failed to write, as he did for a period of two or three months during the summer before he died, he became so distressed, so tense and irritable, that he was a pain to Gertrude and the others at Meadow House, and to his friends as well. I wrote him a letter during that time of blockage in which I told him, as pointedly and eloquently as I could, what he and everyone already knew, viz. that the springs of poetry don't always flow, but they never entirely dry up, either. He was grateful for the letter. He told me he felt lucky to have such a good friend to console him in his old age. But most of the time he was not blocked. He wrote continually, poem after poem, and even if some of them, many of them, were repetitious and predictable, he still regularly turned out brilliantly original images and turns of phrase.

The poetic single-mindedness of Jas in his last years would have astonished Pound, and no doubt plenty of other people whom he knew when he was young. Yet we all know that in old age the individual's primary character comes to the surface, inhibitions fall away and the obsessive impulses emerge. This had nothing, or at least very little, to do with ego or a desire for fame and status; I'm convinced of the purity of artistic ambition in Jas. After all, what did he have to gain by writing poetry? He possessed all the fame and status he could possibly use already. As the years went by, he spent more and more time in the company of the ancients and the great writers of the European Renaissance, he read and reread the old Loeb editions of the classics that he had bought on Harvard Square sixty years before. He lived in Meadow House, where he ate his soft-boiled egg every morning and took off his clothes every night, but far more accurately he lived in the company of beautiful language and cogent thought, in the world of poetic myth that is ultimately so much more substantial than any other world. He wrote because that is what one does in the world of poetic myth. But he took no stock in his capacity to contribute more than a tiny iota, the merest whisper, to the great historical swell of human song.

This is what held us together in our peculiar friendship, the rich man and the poor man, the man of worldly accomplishment and the man of worldly incapacity, the educated sophisticate and the inapt rustic – in short, the aristocrat and the anarchist. In the presence of sublimity we both responded alike, and we acknowledged this to one another tacitly. Nothing else much mattered. The swing of a line by Pound or Shakespeare, the trenchancy of a natural image by Goethe or Ronsard, these were what mattered. As the American twentieth century proceeded ever deeper into political corruption, social demoralization, and economic fatuity, as the qualities of greed and egomania more and more invaded the domain of esthetic consciousness, as pedantry flourished and talent was driven into diaspora, these two friends were overcome together by great sadness. The goodness and beauty they had seen and heard and touched were fading out of the world. History was repeating itself, and they were continually reminded of how fine it would have been to live in the time before our time, the era, say, of Debussy and Proust, Cézanne, the Rhymers' Club, Rilke, and Mann, and all the others whose lost world was elegized by Mauberley in 1919. And it's worth saying that that lost world was also the world of the great socialist revival, William Morris, Bernard Shaw, the Webbs, Kropotkin, Montessori, and in the U.S., Bryan, Gompers, Debs, Wild Bill Haywood,[39] and many others. It was one collapse after another as the twentieth century ran its course, or rather a continuing collapse, like a well that falls in on itself as the water drains away.

So much of our lives had been consumed by this. We'd had

39. Who was the subject of the first book I attempted, written when I was an undergraduate and fortunately never published.

plenty of good times, yes, we were free men and sensualists, we were workers. But the sadness always prevailed.

I remember the evening
that Uncle Willy's bees

swarmed in the neigh-
bor's yard high up in

an old box elder tree
the gravid cluster hung

swelled with so many
thousand bees it al-

most broke the branch
and Uncle Willy sent

his boy Peter up the
trunk with a garbage

pail but of course the
pail fell and the whole

big cluster came down
right on top of Uncle

Willy's head but he
stood still and never

got stung though he
was black with bees so

James Laughlin

Hayden Carruth

for the next two weeks
he was quoting Horace

how a wolf won't bite
so virtuous a man and

after he'd coaxed and
smoked the bees into a

new hive he sat out on
the front porch with his

shoes off and drank 3
highballs down one for

the bees & one for the
dead departed soul of

President Heber Grant
& one to the health

of that dauntless war-
rior General Principles

this all happened just
when the Russians were

blasting Berlin and for
a long time that livid

cluster hung in my mind
the black & burned and

crawling deathshead of
my youth's Old Europe.

This is called "The Swarming Bees." Jas wrote it in about 1946.

Well, let's not get carried away. I'm not addressing the Consuls and Senators here, and the truth is that the Consuls and Senators have all disappeared into the swamp. I don't know who my auditor is, in fact, which is part of the problem. Years ago, in the late 1960s, a dear and wise friend told me that literature would have to wait until "after the revolution."[40] I was dismayed by that thought then, and I am dismayed now. I believed literature was in the service of the revolution, was a part of the revolution. I hope it is. So did Jas. His revolution and mine were doubtless different, and doubtless too neither of us knew what our revolutions were or should be or could be, but we knew they were fueled by the same hope and inspired by the same values.

Whom am I addressing? I think I am addressing those few, those very few, who in their confusing dissimilarities still perceive today that truly extraordinary human minds have lived on earth and that we all are continually reduced by their loss.

Jas died on November 12, 1997.[41] Gertrude called. Then someone from the office in New York called. Then people from all over the country called. I unplugged my phone. I hobbled out to the pasture and pissed in the snow.

---

40. Adrienne Rich, who fortunately for us all did not adhere to her own stricture.
41. On November 17, five days later, my daughter Martha also died.

POSTSCRIPT

On August 19, 1998, I read my poems in Farmington, Connecticut, on the outskirts of Hartford, before a large audience – large for me, at any rate, and indeed large for poetry. In the next day's newspaper the number of people attending was said to have been 2,500. Before and after my reading a good modicum of them approached me. They did not speak of Muriel Rukeyser, Henry Miller, Langston Hughes, Kenneth Rexroth, Tom Merton, Tennessee Williams, Gwendolyn Brooks, Denise Levertov, and Delmore Schwartz. They spoke of names fashionable at the moment, prize-winning nonentities.

Joe-Anne and I had spent the previous afternoon and night in Norfolk. Gertrude was able to sit in an armchair beside her bed, slouched and enervated. She was about three-quarters conscious, I'd say, and about half lucid. We hugged and kissed as well as we could, and she told me how appealing her impending death appeared to her. She said, "I love Jesus first, James second, and you third." A peculiar triumvirate, was what I said to myself.

"You take good care of Hayden," she said to Joe-Anne, "or I'll haunt you."

Meadow House was full of people. Leila and Carlene,[42] Maggie and Sandor, many I didn't know, including doctors and nurses. The dark, brooding portrait of Ann still hung in the guest room. Jas's office was bare. It was a cool summer day, almost but not quite raining, and I was wheezing badly, my eyelids were swollen and heavy. I sat on the terrace and drank coffee and smoked. I looked at the shadblow tree, which stood

42. Mrs. Henry Laughlin, Jas's daughter-in-law.

147

old and twisted in its accustomed place, nearly leafless, looked at the meadow where no sheep ran and the grass was ragged, invaded here and there by patches of goldenrod and hardhack. The birches on the knoll were bent and stained with oozing sap. The fence was broken. The flower beds were overgrown.

In our capital the likes of Clinton and Gingrich were babbling constantly in vulgarese about one another's iniquities, as they still are, while everyone was stuffing themselves with dollars. Old voices – Roosevelt, Baruch, Stevenson, John L. Lewis – sounded faintly in my inner ear.

In my own brief seventy-seven years I have seen the flowering of American civilization, and although we know full well its flaws of injustice and derangement, it was a truly remarkable garden. Now, unmistakably, I saw it withered and fallen.

A week later Leila called me to tell me of Gertrude's death.

I didn't go to Gertrude's funeral. I didn't visit the grave of Jas. Everything I could have known was in my head. And all of it was insufficient.

– H.C.
September 14, 1998

ABOUT THE AUTHOR

In a career spanning six decades, Hayden Carruth has served poetry in every conceivable capacity. His oeuvre includes forty books of poetry and criticism, a novel, and one of the most celebrated and influential anthologies of the last half of this century, *The Voice That Is Great Within Us.*

Hayden Carruth was born in 1921 and for many years lived in northern Vermont. He lives now in upstate New York, where he taught in the Graduate Creative Writing Program at Syracuse University. His most recent books are *Reluctantly, Scrambled Eggs & Whiskey, Selected Essays & Reviews, Collected Shorter Poems: 1946-1991,* and *Collected Longer Poems.*

He has been editor of *Poetry,* poetry editor for *Harper's,* and for more than twenty years an advisory editor for *The Hudson Review.*

Awards

National Book Award in Poetry (1996)
National Book Critics Circle Award in Poetry (1992)
National Book Award Finalist (1992)
Paterson Poetry Prize (1994)
Lenore Marshall/ *The Nation* Poetry Prize (1991)
Guggenheim Foundation Fellowship (twice)
Bollingen Foundation Fellowship
National Endowment for the Arts Senior Fellowship
National Endowment for the Arts Fellowship (three times)
Lannan Literary Fellowship (1995)
Carl Sandburg Award
The Whiting Award
The Ruth Lily Prize
Vermont Governor's Medal

PHOTO CREDITS

The Chinese character for poetry (*shih*) combines *word* and *temple*. It also serves as raison d'être for Copper Canyon Press.

Founded in 1972, Copper Canyon publishes extraordinary work – from Nobel laureates to emerging poets – striving to maintain the highest standards of design, manufacture, marketing, and distribution. Our commitment is nurtured and sustained by the community of readers, writers, booksellers, librarians, teachers, students – everyone who shares the conviction that poetry clarifies and deepens social and spiritual awareness.

Great books depend on great presses. Publication of great poetry is especially dependent on the informed appreciation and generous patronage of readers. By becoming a Friend of Copper Canyon Press you can secure the future – and the legacy – of one of the finest independent publishers in America.

For information and catalogs

COPPER CANYON PRESS
Post Office Box 271
Port Townsend, Washington 98368
360/385-4925
coppercanyon@olympus.net
www.ccpress.org

The typeface used here is Utopia, designed for digital composition by Robert Slimbach in 1989. Utopia has a vertical axis and flat serifs that give it the patrician quality found in neoclassical faces of the eighteenth century. Book design and composition by Valerie Brewster, Scribe Typography. Printed on recycled, acid-free Glatfelter Author's Text at McNaughton & Gunn, Inc.